A Celebration of Steiff

1908

STEIFF
DAS GUTE SPIELZEUG

A Celebration of Steiff

Timeless Toys for Today

Photography by Walter Pfeiffer

Text by Krystyna Poray Goddu

Book Design by John Vanden-Heuvel

A Robert Campbell Rowe Book/Portfolio Press

First Edition/First Printing

Library of Congress Catalog number 97-091676
ISBN 0-942620-19-4

Contents

50

Chapter 1

The Story of Steiff

The 19th-century church bells toll every quarter hour in the picturesque town square in the small German town of Giengen an der Brenz. Down the hill at the Steiff factory, the nimble fingers of local craftspeople fashion felt and mohair into myriad varieties of soft toys that have delighted children and adults throughout the world since 1880. Here is the story, more than a century old, of Steiff toys.

Preceding pages: It all began with an elephant, and the animal has always figured importantly in Steiff's story. The large elephants, from left, are: a pull-along on wheels, circa 1919; a roly poly on a wooden base, circa 1914; a standing white example in a red vest, also circa 1914. The small grey elephant wearing a red blanket was made in 1930 to celebrate Steiff's jubilee, while the tiny white one on a felt rug is an early example, circa 1888.

Right: In 1880 Margarete Steiff made this small felt elephant as a present for her sister-in-law, Anna Steiff.

Below right: In 1889 Fritz Steiff persuaded his sister to move her company out of their parents' home and into this house.

Far into the nineteenth century, in Giengen an der Brenz in south central Germany, a young woman named Margarete Steiff stitched a small elephant from felt. She followed a simple pattern she had found in the fashion magazine *Modenwelt*, then filled the five-inch felt body with lambswool. She was a skillful seamstress who earned her livelihood with her fingers, as she had lost the use of both legs to a bout of polio, which had struck her when she was eighteen months old. For nearly three years, Margarete had been successfully running her own dressmaking company, making felt clothing alongside her employees. But the making of the elephant gave her a special pleasure, and she made many more, in a variety of colors, and gave them to friends and their children, to use as pincushions or playthings.

In 1880, she sold eight of the elephants, and those sales officially mark the beginning of the Margarete Steiff Toy Company. The company's price list of 1883 includes, after a long description of clothing, the offering of "Felt toys for children—robust and safe. Elephant with colored blanket." The elephant was available in a selection of sizes, with or without metal wheels on the feet. The description continues: "The elephant is of soft felt material, which is as supple as leather. The filling is of leftover felt pieces. There is no newer or more desirable child's toy on the market."

Margarete's initial small success with her elephants inspired her brother, Fritz Steiff—a master builder who was married, with six sons and three daughters—to search for greater business opportunities for her company. Fritz took a group of the toy elephants to a market in nearby Heidenheim and obtained many new orders for them. In 1883 he arranged for his sister's products to be displayed in an export showroom in Stuttgart. His sales efforts propelled Margarete and her employees to greater production and variety. Before long they were producing other stuffed toy animals from the patterns that appeared with regularity in *Modenwelt*.

The company was based in the home of Margarete and

Fritz's parents, but Fritz eventually encouraged his sister to move her employees into a larger building. In 1889, the small firm took its place in a new building that boasted a corner shop with two windows in which toys and felt fabric could be displayed. The words *Filz Spielwaaren Fabrik* (Felt Toy Factory) were painted on one wall. The mail-order business flourished, and the number of offerings grew so large that in 1892 Margarete published her first illustrated catalog.

In addition to his efforts at sales and business growth, Fritz helped Margarete with technical problems that arose as her toy production increased. He developed a wooden frame, which eventually became a metal one, to help support the larger animals, whose excelsior-stuffed legs often could not bear their weight. This development led to the manufacture of pull-along and ride-on toys. He also aided his sister in obtaining materials and tools for increasing production. On March 3, 1893, the Margarete Steiff Toy Company was entered in the business register of the Chamber of Commerce, declaring four employees and ten homeworkers. In 1894 the first traveling salesman was hired, and his efforts dramatically increased the number of the company's retail customers.

Eleven-inch-high Jumbo elephant (circa 1930) was the center of attention, but the 3-inch-long mouse (circa 1913) grabbed the limelight. On Jumbo's left, from left: a tiger, 4¾ inches high, circa 1930; a sitting tiger, 7 inches high, circa 1932; a 5½-inch tiger on wheels, circa 1916–1917; a 10-inch-high tiger on wheels, circa 1939, and a 1928 lion, 15½ inches long. On Jumbo's right: a lioness, 7½ inches high, 1948; a lion standing 6¾ inches high, circa 1930; a sitting lion, 6 inches high, circa 1930; a sitting lioness, 6 inches high, circa 1948; a 3¾-inch lion, circa 1930.

Above: These monkeys range from a 4-inch 1908 example, (foreground, riding on a red-capped, red-wheeled pull monkey, circa 1931, 8¾ inches high), to a 16-inch 1908 piece, in a red sweater and cap. Steiff made an 8½-inch roly poly in 1894 (a seated monkey in a red-and-white hat with a white clown ruffle around his neck). The bear-and-monkey rocking wiwag in the right background is circa 1922. Steiff also produced automobile figures, such as these two monkeys wearing chauffeur hats, in 1914.

Right: The front and back covers of the 1892 catalog show the new factory building, as well as some of the characters created by Steiff.

Margarete Steiff focused her efforts on the creation of the felt toys. She sewed every sample herself so that she would have firsthand experience of potential problems the homeworkers might encounter, and so that she could keep a sharp eye out for these weak spots in the finished pieces. From the start, the Steiff toys were distinguished by their materials: wool felt of top quality, stuffed in the first years with lambswool, which was soon replaced by excelsior (fine wood shavings). Some animals were also made of plush (at that time, a velvet-like material woven from wool, cotton, worsted, jute and angora) or, when an especially high quality was desired, from mohair. Occasionally real fur, or a wool weave called krimmer, was used. And early on, the trademark of an elephant identified Steiff toys; at first, it was printed on paper tags worn by the animals.

Eventually competition in the form of cheaply made imitations jolted Margarete into registering patents for her animals. In 1899, the local court in Heidenheim received the first patent registration application from Steiff for twenty-three "soft-filled toys made of cloth." The list of animals included: a velvet deer; a velvet elephant; a velvet fox terrier; a felt fox terrier; a painted velvet rabbit, lying down; a painted velvet rabbit, begging; a painted velvet rabbit head; an elephant on a tricycle; a dancing bear; a monkey portraying a hussar; a monkey portraying an infantryman; a monkey

portraying a coachman; a monkey portraying a Cuban; a painted velvet cat, lying down; a painted velvet cat, sitting; Nansen the explorer with a polar bear; a bear handler with a brown bear; a frog; and a dachshund.

Even before registering her patents, however, Margarete made several decisions that would influence the company's growth and future direction. Since 1893, her toys had been displayed at the Leipzig Spring Fair, an important trade show, by an exhibition company. In 1897, she determined that the time had come to have her own stand. And, even more portentously, she determined that the company would be represented at the Leipzig Fair by her young nephew Richard, Fritz's son. Richard's trip to Leipzig was the beginning of the twenty-year-old man's intense professional involvement with his aunt's company, an involvement that would propel the movement not only of Steiff, but of the international toymaking industry, and enrich the childhoods of girls and boys all over the world.

Richard Steiff had been a creative child, whose artistic talents were recognized by both his aunt and his father. He studied at an art school in Stuttgart, where he produced a large number of sketches and other designs. From his earliest years, he had a special love for bears, and in Stuttgart he indulged himself in sketching them—bears in zoos, circus bears from circuses that performed in Heidenheim and Giengen,

Above: Early in this century, dancing bears wearing muzzles were a common sight in towns throughout Europe. They were led by a chain attached to a ring in the nose.

Above left: Among the earliest animals made by the Steiffs were dancing bears. This 1898 toy, complete with chain and stick, is a roly poly on a wooden base; it stands 13 inches (including base).

Left: Otto Steiff, in the foreground, checks a packing list in the light and airy shipping room at the factory, circa 1903–1904.

Following pages: From left in photo, these bear cubs are a sampling of the variety Steiff has created: circa 1954, 5½ inches; circa 1957, 8½ inches; circa 1908, 6½ inches, originally on wheels; circa 1906, 10 inches and on wheels; circa 1934, 5 inches.

Above: This photo illustrates the novelties offered by Steiff at the Leipzig Spring Fair in 1903. It is also the only existing documentation, shadowy as it is, of the first Steiff bear.

Right: The first "button-in-ear," used in 1904–1905, featured an elephant.

Opposite page: The earliest teddy bears in the Steiff archives are, from left: an 18-inch golden teddy stuffed with kapok, circa 1905, jointed with paper discs and short metal rods; the 1904 Bärle, 15 inches high, stuffed with excelsior, featuring a long snout, long arms, a sealing-wax nose and paper-disc joints with string; the grey 1905 Richard Steiff Bärle, 11½ inches, stuffed with excelsior and featuring a stitched nose. Most similar of the three to today's teddy bears, Bärle also has paper-disc joints on short metal rods.

dancing bears that performed in the city streets with traveling gypsies. Private family correspondence and notes suggest that as early as the 1890s Richard was already thinking of creating a cuddly toy for boys, and that his love for bears directed his creative process towards the idea that such a toy should be a bear. As psychologically astute as he was artistically creative, Richard recognized that in an era that celebrated militarism and stereotypical male virtues, boys needed something soft to cuddle and hug when they were feeling low. He was astute enough to realize, too, that a doll would not do. During his student life, the seed of the teddy bear was taking root in Richard Steiff's spirit, although it would be many more years before it was to blossom.

Richard's representation of Steiff at the Leipzig Spring Fair was highly successful. He took many orders, established international contacts, and convinced his aunt that further expansion was necessary. Richard's own personal talents and interests led him to concentrate on the design and production of new soft toys, especially animals, but he was involved in some way in most aspects of the business for many years.

The next year, 1898, two of Richard's brothers joined him in the company: Paul, born in 1876, who was also artistic and had studied with Richard at art school in Stuttgart, and Franz, born in 1878, who specialized in weaving. Paul had worked at Steiff during school holidays, and Margarete asked him to join the pattern department at the company. He also sketched animals, and later took over the departments of design and quality control. Franz used his weaving skills in the production of plush animals, and eventually became responsible for buying materials and establishing the overseas warehouses, as well as organizing branches of the company within Germany to supervise the homeworkers. He is credited with developing the "button-in-ear" trademark for which Steiff became (and remains) so widely known.

In 1902 another brother, Otto, joined the company. Born in 1885, he had studied business in Cologne; he actively established Steiff in other countries over the years, including the United States. The year 1903 was important, too, for being the beginning of the construction, in a joint family venture, of three new factory buildings (1903, 1904 and 1908).

Above: Margarete Steiff, at her desk, is holding a felt cat rattle in her left hand.

Above right: In 1909 Richard Steiff posed with his prototype teddy bear for this English publicity photo.

Below right: Dating from the period of 1907–1913, these three bears illustrate the teddy trends of those years. From left: a rare black bear, circa 1907, has red stitching and a sealing wax nose (Steiff would not make a black bear again until 1912); a white 6½-inch snap-apart bear was made in 1909; the Dolly Bear, 11 inches high, was made in a variety of colors in 1913 and was especially popular in the United States.

Richard initiated the designs for the new buildings, which were the focus of a great deal of widespread attention, as they were highly original and, architecturally speaking, years ahead of their time. Still in use today, they are long and flat, and stand two to three stories high, with double glass walls, constructed to allow as much light as possible inside. They are regarded as precursors to the work of later famous architects such as Walter Gropius and Mies van der Rohe.

When it was time for the second new building at Steiff, Hugo Steiff, another of Fritz's sons, then a student of mechanical engineering at the School of Engineering in Mannheim, was called upon to design it. In 1906, Hugo officially joined the company, taking on the responsibility of all future building projects.

Meanwhile, the production of toys was continuing at a rapid pace. Between 1897 and 1899, Richard designed many new animals based on his sketches from the Stuttgart Zoo. His brother Paul's technical knowledge helped turn the designs into three-dimensional animals. The brothers learned that the stuffing stage of production was crucial, for it was the stuffing that literally shaped the animals, giving them the true-to-life appearance of their counterparts at the zoo, or in the wild.

Richard's love for bears led the company to produce a large variety in the 1890s: bears in different sizes and colors; with or without growlers; pull-along bears on all fours on metal wheels; and a dancing bear on two legs with a chain and

stick, balanced on a rounded wooden base. By the end of 1902, again using his zoo sketches as guidelines, Richard developed simple movable joints—often just attached to the body by string—for many of the animals, rendering them even more true-to-life.

In February 1903, Paul Steiff took five wooden crates of sample toys to a showroom in New York, where he was to promote the sale of Steiff toys in the United States. Among these toys was a new large plush bear known as "Bär 55 PB." The name indicates that the bear (Bär) was plush (P), jointed (B—for *beweglich*, which means jointed in German) and fifty-five centimeters (twenty-one-and-a-half inches) high, sitting. Americans considered the toys too expensive and they were not well received. The new bear in particular was regarded not only as too expensive, but also too big and heavy to have any appeal as a child's plaything. According to Richard Steiff's later comments, his aunt was not surprised at this failure—she had predicted that the bear would be too

These four record bears are pull-along toys on wooden wagons with wheels. From left: a 5-inch golden bear, circa 1926; a 5-inch red tipped bear, circa 1924; a 1928 record Petsy, 9½ inches high; a 7-inch Rosy, circa 1913.

Right: Sailors were popular throughout the entire early production of dolls at Steiff. These three illustrate the evolution of the figure from the primitive, far left, in 1905, which stands about 12½ inches high, through the move towards realism in 1916, center, and the most refined, right, in 1936. (The two later sailors are each about 13½ inches high.)

Below right: He looks like Humpty Dumpty, and this 1906 doll *is* modeled after the nursery-rhyme figure, but copyright laws prevented Steiff from calling him by his rightful name. Instead, they dubbed him the Märsbewohner, or man from Mars.

Opposite page: After Richard Steiff's move to the United States in 1923, he began to call for friendlier bears. The factory responded with bears like Petsy, at left, in 1928, who is meant to resemble a baby bear. This example is 13 inches high. In 1929, the 11-inch blue bear represented a new type of bear. Smiling and often dressed, it was made with a closed or open mouth.

expensive to be popular.

The next month, the bear was shown at the Spring Fair in Leipzig, where it met with similar disinterest. But at the last minute, as the disappointed Steiff brothers were packing up, an equally disappointed American buyer, Hermann Berg from Geo. Borgfeldt & Co. in New York, stopped by the Steiff stand. Disgruntled and unhappy that he had not found anything new at the Fair, he asked Richard Steiff if the company could design a soft, cuddly new toy for his firm. Richard Steiff handed him one of the heretofore unpopular bears. Hermann Berg, in a pivotal moment for the toymaking industry, declared his attraction to the bear and ordered three thousand.

While the order is known to have been filled and shipped, any other record of these three thousand bears has disappeared. There is no Bär 55 PB in the Steiff Museum in Giengen, and no prototype has ever turned up and been identified. Since the "button-in-ear" identification was not yet in place, the bears have no identifying marks. The only record of this first Bär 55 PB is a blurry catalog photograph (see page 18), which shows only a dark, plump shape. A record of pattern registration for a jointed bear at the Court of Heidenheim on July 13, 1903, does exist.

Acknowledging the general lack of interest in Bär 55 PB, yet still optimistic about the potential appeal of a stuffed bear, Richard Steiff attempted to

Just prior to World War I and throughout the war years, Steiff created a wide array of international soldiers, all of them felt and about 14 inches high. This sampling includes, from left: a Russian soldier, a French Zoave, an Italian carabiniere, a Turkish soldier, the English "Tommy" (who is earlier than the others, dating from 1911), a German artillery man, an Italian soldier and a French soldier.

better his toy. With all the criticisms in mind, he made the design smaller and less plump, improved the joints, and used a light-colored mohair plush. The arms and snout were still long; the nose was still formed by sealing wax. While the changes made the bear less true-to-life, they rendered it more appealing. In March 1904, the new model was registered as "Bär 35 PB" (about fourteen inches, sitting).

Richard's younger brother Franz was sent to sell this newer bear at the World's Fair in St. Louis. His trip, unlike Paul's to New York the year before, was a great success. Richard's improvements had the desired result. Not only did the company sell 12,000 bears that year, but Richard and Margarete Steiff received Gold Medals and the Grand Prix Award. The foundation for Steiff's future reputation was laid. With such a popular item in their line, it was more crucial than ever that the Steiffs find a means of identifying, and thus protecting,

their original creations. So it was that in 1904, the elements most associated with Steiff today were established: the cuddly, soft bear and the "button-in-ear" identification.

Franz Steiff came up with the idea of inserting a button in the ear of each toy animal as a more permanent identification tool than paper labels, which had been used up to that time. The very first toys had small blank buttons, but the company quickly decided that the buttons should be embossed with the company logo: the elephant with an "s"-shaped trunk. Margarete Steiff announced this innovation as a legally protected trademark in a newsletter, explaining: "As of November 1, 1904, I shall identify each article without exception, with a small nickel-plated button in the left ear. Our logo is stamped on these buttons and is legally protected." When the German patent office determined that a button inserted in the ear of a toy could not be legally protected, the company chose, instead, to patent the words "button-in-ear." This patent was accepted and legally confirmed on May 13, 1905.

In the midst of these patenting decisions, the evolution of what would soon become known as the teddy bear was in progress. The successful Bär 35 PB and a smaller version, Bär 28 PB, which was about eleven inches, sitting, were made and sold throughout 1904 and much of 1905. Although the bear was selling, the Steiff family was not pleased with it. They felt the bear

Far left: The American explorer Robert E. Peary's 1909 North Pole expedition inspired Steiff to create a series of Eskimo dolls, both white and dark skinned. These two are about 14 inches high; the dark-skinned one is circa 1908 and the fair-skinned one dates from 1910.

Left: This 1905 English policeman, 19 inches high, is an early, still rather primitive, character doll.

Above left: Like the rest of the factory, the Steiff warehouse was also a light and airy space.

Following pages: Steiff has produced practically every breed of dog, as well as some born of imagination. A small representation includes, from left in photo: Cheerio, a laughing puppy, 6½ inches high, circa 1929; a 7-inch poodle, circa 1914; a 10-inch German shepherd, circa 1926; a 9¼-inch Dalmatian, circa 1932; the bloodhound Treff, standing 6½ inches high, adapted in 1928 from an English Dalmatian called Dismal Desmond made by Dean's Rag Book; a 7-inch fox terrier, circa 1930; Troll, 6½ inches high, circa 1936; and a 7½-inch boxer, which was made from 1947–1953.

Schäferhund

Treff
Troll

still did not appeal enough to children, but nobody seemed to have a clear idea of how to better the design. Richard Steiff, however, did not give up, and continued to design a number of variations. The one he finally showed Margarete early in 1905 pleased her greatly. It, too, was thirty-five centimeters, but its overall look was much rounder and softer. It was filled with excelsior and kapok, which made it lighter than the earlier bears; the face was rounder; the nose was less pointed and was stitched, rather than shaped with sealing wax. Most importantly, it was disc-jointed, as Steiff bears have been since then. Instead of using wires or metal rods to attach the limbs, Richard designed heavy round cardboard discs to be placed inside the limbs and body. These were held together by a metal pin. The effect was that of a doll-like stuffed bear with movable joints.

This bear was registered on February 12, 1905, as Bär 35 PAB, and became known as Bärle (an affectionate way of saying "little bear"). Bärle was made in several sizes ranging from ten inches to forty-five inches and in several colors of mohair: dark brown, light brown and white. Of course it had the elephant button in the left ear. But by 1905–1906, the elephant had given way to the words "STEIFF" printed on the button. Sometimes the bear had a squeeze-box voice made of leather with a mechanical movement. When the

Above: In the 1930s the fat-cheeked Teddy-Baby was popular. This group includes: a 16-inch open-mouth brown example; a 12½-inch white one; and three from 3½ to 7 inches, two with open mouths.

Opposite page: In 1909, Steiff made their first Max and Moritz dolls, based on Wilhelm Busch's popular cartoons. These two, center, are 12 inches high, circa 1910. Surrounding them, from left, are 17-inch characters: Uncle Fritz, Widow Bolte, Teacher Lampel, Mrs. Bock and Tailor Bock, circa 1915–1917.

Left: Other storybook characters included Dr. Heinrich Hoffmann's Struwwelpeter in 1912 (14 inches) and Florence Upton's Golliwogg in 1910 (13 inches).

Right: In 1936 Steiff tried to revive its doll program with a line of figures with pressed-felt faces, such as this clown.

Below right: In the early 1920s, Albert Schlopsnies designed a line of celluloid dolls. Rolf, made in 1922 and 15 inches high, is a typical example. He wears a red label reading: Steiff-Schlopsnies Puppe. The line was unsuccessful and was eliminated in 1925.

Opposite page: Ever pushing further in its pursuit of the friendly—and less expensive—teddy, Steiff came up with Dicky-Bear, with a smiling face and painted paws. The 14-inch golden example is a well-made mohair Dicky-Bear, circa 1931. By 1938, expense and shortage of materials had begun to affect production. The 13-inch brown Dicky-Bear dates from that year; it is wool plush and has no painting on its paws.

belly of the animal was pressed, the voice sounded. (In 1908 many of the bears got an automatic growler, with the growl activated when the animal was tilted forward.)

Bärle was the bear the Steiffs had been hoping for. Its appeal was immediate and strong. The factory expanded and the number of homeworkers grew dramatically, spreading throughout the Giengen area to reach a number of 1,800 by 1907. Even with this expansion, Steiff could hardly fill all the orders that came in from within Germany and from the United States, where the demand for the stuffed bears was especially great, and is credited to then-president Teddy Roosevelt.

While several stories exist as to exactly why the stuffed bear came to be linked to Roosevelt, there is no dispute that a strong connection exists. The best-known story linking stuffed toy bears with Roosevelt is as follows: In November 1902 the cartoonist Clifford K. Berryman drew a cartoon that was published in *The Washington Post*. Berryman depicted Roosevelt on a hunting expedition, presented with a bear cub on a leash, for the president's shooting pleasure. In the cartoon, Roosevelt is turning away from the bear, waving his hand in refusal. The caption reads: "Drawing the Line in Mississippi." Berryman continued to use the popular bear cub in his cartoons, and the Steiff bear became known first as Teddy's bear and by 1906 as, simply, the teddy bear.

There are many unconfirmed anecdotes about the role the teddy bear played in the public and private life of the Roosevelts. It is uncontested, however, that teddy-bear mania swept across the United States in the early years of this century, and that Steiff was the major producer of the stuffed teddy bears. Other German firms quickly began to

Made in
Germany

STEIFF · ORIGINAL · MARKE
Minnie Mouse
Copyright by Walt Disney
Micky Mouse
Micky Mouse

Opposite page: From 1931 until 1936, Steiff had the German license to produce the popular cartoon character Mickey Mouse. Minnie was also made, starting in 1932; this example stands 8½ inches high. The Mickeys range from 6 to 15 inches high and are all early examples from 1931 and 1932.

Left: The four bears in this photo illustrate the post-war design transition. From left: in 1940 a small number of bears were made of rayon. This 18-inch green rayon teddy still looks like the older Steiff bears, as does the straw-colored wool plush bear from 1952, which is 14 inches high and retains the rounder head and longish arms of the old form. The larger (18-inch) golden mohair bear, though, was also made in 1952 but is beginning to look more like the teddy of the future. Finally, the 1966 bear on the far right, 20 inches, is unmistakably new in style, with the "mask" around its facial features. This style was made until the early 1990s.

copy this popular toy; American firms began making teddy bears between 1906 and 1907. At first these firms, both German and American, advertised that their bears were exact reproductions of Steiff's unbreakable soft toys, at lower prices. Thanks to her registered patents, Margarete Steiff was able to put a stop to the claims. The production of the competing bears continued but only Steiff bears had the distinguishing "button-in-ear." The careful buyer could easily identify a Steiff bear. Still, over the next few years, Margarete Steiff had to fight many legal battles from German competitors such as Wilhelm Strunz, Deuerlein and Gebruder Bing, who attempted to confuse buyers by adopting similar trademarks. Their attempts ranged from creating a "ring-in-ear" trademark to securing a paper tag in each animal's left ear with a metal button to placing a metal button in the *right* ear. All of these competing trademarks were eventually legally prevented from use. Sometimes, Steiff even adopted their ideas; for example, after Strunz gave up using a stapled tag in

the left ear, Steiff decided to fix a small cloth tag, printed with the name, product number and symbol of each animal, in the ear with the metal button. (This is still the method of identification used.)

As the legal battles raged, teddy bear production continued. Certain elements and innovative variations disappeared and reappeared; the toy's identifying shape and characteristics evolved. Richard Steiff's 1905 Bärle, first made as a small grey bear, resembled the teddy bear we know today as a standard, traditional teddy. Between Bärle and today's variety of teddy bear styles came a wide range of innovations. In 1907, for example, a dramatic black bear with red stitching and a sealing-wax nose was made. (Steiff would not make another black bear until 1912, and most bears after Bärle had stitched noses.) In 1909, deciding to give in to children's desire to take off their dolls' and animals' limbs during play, the company manufactured toys with snap-apart arms, legs, and heads. A snap-apart teddy bear was produced that year, as well as a golliwogg and other roly-poly toys, which could be rolled around like a ball when the limbs and head were taken off. (All the body parts could be easily re-fastened with the same snaps, of course, when the child wanted his or her old toy back

in its original form.) Glass eyes became available in place of shoe-button eyes; the range of colors available expanded from white, beige and dark brown to include gold and black. In 1913, the colorful "Bär Dolly" (Dolly Bear) was produced in red, white and blue, to commemorate the 1912 United States elections. (Yellow and green Bär Dollys were also made.) The bear's head was always white, and it had a colorful neck ruff, and a voice box that was activated by squeezing.

In 1908 the company was stunned by the sudden death—the result of an accident—of Franz Steiff. This important member of the Steiff team was only thirty years old. The family and the company had barely recovered from their grief when a second tragedy struck: on May 9, 1909, Margarete Steiff, their guiding force, died. She was two months shy of her sixty-second birthday, and not only Steiff, but the entire toy world mourned her.

These two deaths briefly immobilized the company, but the nephews were determined to persevere. They appointed Hugo and Otto as managing directors, while Richard and Paul maintained their roles as the creative leaders of the company.

Looking to the future without Margarete or Franz, the remaining brothers agreed that the continued success of the teddy bear was paramount to the growth of Steiff. The teddy bear inspired many books and stories, and as these began to appear, the company responded in

Opposite page: The character of Coloro the clown was part of Albert Schlopsnies' spectacular circus display. Three original 1911 Coloros stand here with a 1987 replica, who wears a bright blue outfit. Seated by them is August the clown, created in 1916. All the clowns are 17 inches high.

Left: Who's going into the woods? A sampling of Steiff's woodland animals through the decades includes: a red fox, circa 1914; a pull-rabbit on red wooden wheels, circa 1928, and a sitting rabbit dating from 1929; a circa-1934 squirrel; a mountain goat, circa 1937; a deer dating from 1938; a circa-1952 turkey; a standing hedgehog, circa 1951, and one lying down, circa 1961; a marmot dating from 1960; an elk, circa 1963; an owl dating from 1971 and a circa-1985 beaver.

This 10-inch dressed rabbit is a 1929 creation.

Original
Steiff
KNOPF IM OHR

Opposite page: If one black cat is bad luck, what are seven black velvet cats? Very desirable, it seems, since Steiff produced them in many sizes for many decades. This menacing group includes: circa 1914, 11 inches; circa 1920, 14 inches; circa 1950, 6 inches; circa 1936, 3½ inches; circa 1973, 13 inches; circa 1914, 9 inches.

Left: Dachshunds of all sizes have been popular since the early years of this century. These two, 8 inches high and 3 inches high, both date from 1908. The larger one can be pulled along on its cast-iron wheels; one wheel is missing.

turn with bears that fulfilled the literary expectations. For example, in 1907–1908, teddies in striped sweaters matched Seymour Eaton's series *The Roosevelt Bears—Travel and Adventures*. A complete line of dressed bears, garbed in period bathing suits, sailor dresses, pants with suspenders and rompers, followed them. Also in 1907, a bear with a hollow stomach and lace-up front seam was sold with a metal hot-water bottle. The company expected children would put the hot water inside the bear, then lace it up and take it to bed on cold nights. In 1908, bears with muzzles were the novelties of the season.

While Steiff focused a great deal of attention on the teddy bear in the first decades of this century, a large number of other toys—primarily, but not only, soft ones—continued to be developed, produced and sold. Richard Steiff's love of flying led him to invent the Roloplan, a kind of model kite without a tail, which could also be used for aerial photography; it won numerous prizes. Richard's and his brothers' interest in technology prompted

Sounds like a barnyard around here! You could easily start your own Steiff farm, as this 1909 Bavarian couple (12½ inches high) appears to have done. Their holdings include: a circa-1937 horse, 13 inches high; a 12-inch donkey, circa 1933; a pull-goat, 11½ inches, circa 1928, and an 8½-inch goat, circa 1934; a 20-inch goose family on wooden wheels, in the foreground, circa 1920s; two pull-lambs, one 8¾ inches, circa 1935, the other 7 inches and circa 1938; a 6-inch pig, circa 1920; three cows, ranging from 1914 to 1938; an 8½-inch rooster, circa 1926; a 1933 duck, 7 inches high; a 4½-inch pull-duck, circa 1934–35; a 6-inch hatted goose, circa 1928; a colorful felt chicken, 5 inches high, circa 1926; a 7-inch chicken, circa 1930; a 5½-inch duck, circa 1932; and a 3¾-inch chick, circa 1938.

archives at the factory in Giengen also reveals alphabetically-arranged shelf after shelf of elephants, cats, dogs, rabbits, farm animals, woodland creatures and wild beasts in a seemingly infinite range of sizes and variations: with and without wheels, voice boxes and clockwork mechanisms; standing, sitting, lying, begging. And just as some teddy bears came to be modeled after storybooks, so did some of the other animals, for example, Puss in Boots from *Grimm's Fairy Tales* and Beatrix Potter's Peter Rabbit. Large ride-on animals were offered from about 1898 onwards, and were produced with the aid of the neighboring Märklin Toy Company, which helped attach the metal bases and wheels. By 1913, children

Above: "Do you want to know a secret?" A 14½-inch kangaroo from 1933 whispers in the ear of an earlier generation. The grey kangaroo, approximately 12 inches, is circa 1914.

Below right: In 1953 Steiff created Jackie to celebrate fifty years of teddy bear production, and abandoned the old style of teddy. A 6½-inch and 10-inch Jackie encircle 18-inch Zotty, which was made beginning in the 1950s. This example, circa 1959, has long mohair and an open mouth.

Opposite page: Jungle animals were popular in the 1960s and 1970s. The 10-inch zebra is circa 1960; the 19-inch giraffe dates from 1969; the ocelot is 15 inches long, circa 1964, while the gazelle, 7½ inches high, dates from 1975.

them to be the first family in Giengen to buy a car, which in turn led them to create new "automobile" animals and dolls in 1913. These innovative items were first designed to sit atop radiator caps and eventually were used as automobile head-lamp covers; especially popular were chimpanzees wearing chauffeur's caps, but many other animals were created in this form, including bears, elephants, donkeys, pigs, kangaroos and several breeds of dogs.

The mainstay of Steiff production in the years leading up to World War I, however, were the soft animals, which were first made of felt and velvet and later of a fur-like plush. During that era, the most popular animal after the teddy bear was the monkey. A visit through the Steiff

Original Steiff
Original Steiff
Ozelot

could steer the wheeled ride-on toys, thanks again to help from Märklin. In 1914 Steiff developed its own light and quiet wooden wheels to replace the heavy iron ones in use. (In the 1920s, these fine but expensive wooden wheels were in turn replaced by metal, disc-type wheels.)

In addition to the felt elephants and monkeys, velvet dachshunds and black cats, Easter bunnies and myriad other animals with realistic movable joints, Steiff produced its own distinctive lines of dolls. While the very first were produced early in the company's history, around 1892, these were apparently disappointing, with porcelain heads (probably made by other German manufacturers), felt bodies and costumes.

The first series of character dolls—the droll, often comic figures now associated with Steiff—were designed upon Richard's insistence, in 1903, for warm and lively dolls. The redesigns had velvet faces, shoe-button eyes, painted facial features and velvet or felt bodies with movable joints. They represented policemen, postmen, football players and comic renderings of townspeople. Their felt costumes were not removable, but were an integral part of their bodies. Most, but not all, had a seam down the middle of the face, and many character child dolls also had horizontal seams that ran from the outside edge of each eye to the ear, which enhanced the potential for shaping and refining the faces. By 1904, the dolls included charac-

Before, and together with, teddies, polar bears have been a steady part of the company's collection. These four, ranging in height from 4 inches to 7 inches, span the century. The tiniest is a 1987 replica of a 1909 bear; moving up in size, the bears date from 1923, 1939 and 1914.

Cosy Siam
Steiff

Cats appeared in the Steiff catalogs as early as 1892. Here a group of newcomers question their felt ancestor. From left: Tabsy, circa 1960, is about 6¾ inches high; this off-white kitty is circa 1932; Fiffy, circa 1955, is in a typical cat's curl, lying down; Cosy the Siamese cat, circa 1973, measures a full 11 inches to the tip of her tail; the 4-inch felt cat on a felt rug is circa 1908; Tabby is circa 1948.

ters from international children's books and cartoons of the day, such as the Katzenjammer Kids and Happy Hooligans, Mother Hubbard, Buster Brown and His Dog Tige, Florence Upton's golliwogg, Heinrich Hoffmann's Struwwelpeter, Wilhelm Busch's Max and Moritz, and an American Uncle Sam. Finally, in the years immediately preceding World War I, the company produced an enormous range of international soldiers in authentic uniforms. The soldiers originally had comic faces, but as the war neared, customers grew sensitive to the look of these dolls and humor on the subject was no longer appropriate. Dolls were an enormously significant part of the Steiff toy production from 1903 to 1914, and helped form the company's international reputation as a premier toymaker during those years.

Doll and soft-toy production dwindled during the World War I years of 1914–1918. Steiff's growth slowed and eventually stopped altogether, as three company directors, Richard, Paul and Hugo, were all called to serve in the armed forces. By 1916, all borders were closed and export was impossible. Orders came for Steiff to produce supplies for the war effort. The factory was filled with women workers and the homeworkers continued at

their tasks. Though slowed, however, toy production did not cease; it merely altered its direction. Felt was impossible to come by, since all felt produced was destined for the military. Instead the company focused on making wooden toys and military items for children; in addition, a small collection of toys was produced in a material called paper-plush.

A key figure during the war years at Steiff was the Munich artist Albert

new toy and doll designs. Among the spectacular displays he created, sometimes involving as many as 220 dolls, were scenes like "Noah's Ark," "Fire in Zipfelhausen," "The Market" and possibly the best known, the circus dioramas. These were usually shown in prestigious toy-shop windows, as well as at trade-show exhibitions. Among his doll designs, Schlopsnies included Native Americans, Eskimos, blacks, cowboys, sailors, and clowns, as well as dolls representing other nationalities. Responding to the wartime shortage of felt, he developed the celluloid-head doll, which was manufactured from 1921 to 1925.

Opposite page: These three 6-inch-high dressed animals, circa 1969, are part of a German bedtime tradition. Parents would place a sweet under their wide skirts, and place the *betthupferl* by the child's bed to entice the child to "hop into bed." (The German word breaks into two: *bett* meaning bed and *hupferl* meaning to leap.)

Left: In the 1950s Steiff began to reproduce many of the popular dressed animals from earlier decades. Called Puppbär and Puppfuchs (Doll-bear and Doll-fox), this group stands about 9 inches high.

Schlopsnies, who worked closely with the firm beginning in 1910. Schlopsnies was never actually an employee, but his contributions to the company were vast. He was responsible for Steiff's advertising displays, which may well be the best toyland fantasies in history; shop-window displays; posters; printed advertising; exhibitions and dioramas, as well as many

Once the war was over, Steiff struggled back to its feet. By 1922, more buildings were constructed at the factory, and Hugo Steiff brought the conveyor belt into use to speed up production. Mohair animals became more popular than felt and eventually, as modernization of the factory continued, plush animals became the standard. Instead of producing so many ride-on animals, Steiff began to make scooters, tricycles and pedal cars. Discouraged by its inability to sell the comic dolls that had been so successful before World War I and by the unpopularity of the Schlopsnies dolls, the company all but eliminated dolls from its production in 1925. Only gnomes and dwarfs

While Steiff is celebrated for their soft toys, the company has always created a large variety of other playthings, as well. Their wooden pull toys include, from left: lion, circa 1963, 7¼ inches high; horse, circa 1957, 7 inches high; horse and wagon, circa 1937, 4½ inches high; duck, 7¼ inches high, circa 1920. The 4½-inch turtle, circa 1975, is on wheels.

were sold in the second half of the 1920s. (In 1936 an attempt was made to produce child dolls with pressed-felt faces, but these, too, proved unpopular and were produced for only a few years. Steiff abandoned dolls as a serious part of their production until the replica program was started in 1987.)

The soft-toy production, however, took off strongly again after World War I with new designs and other innovations. The muted, realistic coloring of the animals was replaced by strong bright colors. Dogs replaced monkeys—and even teddy bears!—as the most popular animal, appealing to adults as well as to children. Steiff made dogs of every breed in previously unthinkable colors like lavender, orange and green.

The company's biggest hit of all was a plush dog named Molly, which was adapted from a popular design by the English toy company J.K. Farnell. Molly was made from 1925 through the 1950s in every conceivable position and size. Steiff went on to develop a Molliette in 1927, adapted from the English Chad Valley Toy Company's Tango Puppy, a dancing dog with extra-long legs. The body was a replica of the Chad Valley body, while the heads were taken from Molly and other popular Steiff dogs. Aptly capturing the spirit of the Roaring Twenties, the lanky, floppy toys were sold as boudoir and automobile dolls, as well as toys for children.

The jointed "record" animals, which Steiff had been manufacturing since 1912, took on a new life after World War I. The original record animals were seated on a metal chassis with four wheels and held a metal rod. When the toy was pulled along by its attached cord the animal moved back and forth, giving the impression that it was steering itself. The post-war models had clockwork mechanisms that allowed the animals to cycle around by themselves for short periods of time. Other variations were also produced, such as cycles with side cars and two-animal "wiwags" with see-saw-like movements.

With the company's renewed post-war growth, Richard Steiff, hoping to be of more use to the export and marketing divisions of the company, decided in 1923 to emigrate with his family to the United States. Richard took Schlopsnies with him to establish the United States office, but this arrangement was not successful. By 1924, Schlopsnies had returned to Germany and severed his connection with Steiff, much to the company's relief. While the artist's talent and creativity had been welcome, he consistently ran up huge debts and caused other serious financial problems. (A few

Who says we're all wet? These animals love nothing better than to be by the water's edge—or under its surface. The three fish, all called Flossy and either 2 inches or 4 inches high, date from 1969; Lizzy the lizard, 12 inches long, is circa 1959. The 4-inch-high velvet frog is circa 1953, and the 4½-inch-high walrus is circa 1959. The penguin, standing 4¾ inches high, dates from 1960, while both the 3-inch turtle and the 4½-inch seal (Robby) are circa 1974. Mockie the 4-inch hippopotamus was made in 1975.

years after Richard's move, in 1927, the youngest Steiff brother, Ernst, returned to Giengen from the United States, where he had been working as an electrical engineer for fourteen years, and joined the company.)

In the post-war years, the teddy bear continued to be a focus of creative development. From the United States, Richard called for a new emphasis on softness, friendliness and color. The traditional, hard, excelsior-stuffed teddy had become difficult to sell, so Steiff turned to softer, kapok-filled bears. As the shortage of mohair continued, plush teddy bears became the standard, often in colors like gold and pink. When mohair was again more widely available, a longer-haired variety was put into use, often tipped with color. Most of the teddy bears now had glass eyes with black pupils. In 1926, a teddy clown, with tipped mohair, wearing a clown's hat and two-color ruff, was patented in the United States. In 1928, a new friendlier bear design was created: Petsy, who was made to resemble a baby bear cub. It was followed by Teddy-Baby in 1929, a smiling (and eventually, laughing) bear cub, designed at the urging of Richard Steiff. Dicky, designed simultaneously with Teddy-Baby, was an effort to produce a friendly, happy, but cheaper, bear. Its distinguishing feature was its painted paw pads. Originally made in mohair, by 1938 a cheaper model was made in wool plush with no painting. All of Steiff's new bears were produced in the usual range of sizes.

Richard sent frequent reports from the United States on the American toy industry, analyses of Steiff products and ideas for new ones. His correspondence unceasingly stressed the importance of quality control in maintaining the reputation of Steiff toys, and his vantage point was a useful one for the company. Sales in the United States improved dramatically in the years after his arrival, thanks both to his suggestions and to the increased radio and print advertising he promoted.

The principal hindrance to sales the company had always faced was the high price of its carefully made toys. When the economic depression hit the United States in 1929, Richard issued many warnings to the company regarding the need to cut costs in order to lower prices. The economic problems combined in the 1930s with the mounting of anti-German sentiment as Hitler came to greater and greater power, and Steiff found it nearly impossible to get any orders in the United States.

As the 1930s drew to an end and war seemed inevitable, the company began to recognize the approach, again, of wartime problems. The Hitler regime removed both Hugo and Ernst Steiff from their positions and replaced them with its own managers. Production became focused on war articles. Bracing itself for the difficulty of the coming years, the company was hit by an unexpected blow: the death of Richard Steiff, in the United States, on March 31, 1939. Richard died of a heart attack at the age of sixty-three, less than six months before the official start of World War II.

In May 1943 toy production, already at a minimum, stopped completely. Steiff became a factory for producing military equipment. The next year, in February 1944, Otto Steiff died. When the war came to an end, in 1945, nothing remained of the company as it had been known

Opposite page: In the 1960s and 1970s, Steiff made the very soft Cosy Teddy of dralon. All had open mouths and a contrasting color under their necks. In this group, the 8-inch white bear is marked 1967; the others, ranging in size from 8 inches to 15½ inches, are all circa 1968.

Left: In 1994, Steiff introduced a replica of the 1904 Onkel Sam figure, 20 inches high.

Right: The first dolls to be re-created in the company's replica program in 1987 were these two Schlopsnies designs: Betty the tennis player from 1913 is 17 inches high, and the 1914 Gentleman in morning coat is 18 inches high.

Opposite page: Three teddy bears of recent production illustrate the popular styles of the past two decades. From left: the 10½-inch yellow Petsy is circa 1971; a very soft minky Zotty, 12 inches, is circa 1987; and the original Steiff teddy, 14½ inches, was a new, though short-lived, design in 1991.

except, miraculously, its extensive archives, which had been packed into wooden crates, stored outside the factory complex and, somehow, escaped notice. (The archives contain examples of thousands of items Steiff manufactured and continue today to serve as a living history and inspiration for new work.)

It was several years before toy production at Steiff was in full swing again. Many popular pre-war designs were offered, including the pull-along toys and ride-on animals, as well as, of course, the teddy bear, which underwent significant post-war design changes. The face grew rounder; the arms and legs were shortened. In the 1950s and 1960s, mohair and wool-plush teddies were joined by softer, floppier models, made of new materials such as dralon.

Dolls with pressed vinyl heads were added in the 1950s and one of the most popular characters ever was also created during this decade: the German cartoon character Mecki. The hedgehog had been created as a cartoon by Ferdinand Diehl in 1940, but did not hit the heights of popularity until after the war. Steiff obtained the rights to produce a Mecki doll in 1951 and quickly determined that the creature could not be produced with a felt head. Mecki and Mrs. Mecki were introduced in 1951 with rubber-like latex heads. Mrs. Mecki eventually became Micki, and their children, Macki and Mucki, with five-inch-high rubber bodies, were introduced in 1953. (In 1962, the rubber heads and bodies were replaced by the more durable vinyl.) These popular characters are still made today in a range of sizes.

Steiff has always been a toy company, crafting the best play-

STEIFF-ORIGINAL-MARKE
Original
Steiff
Original
Steiffteddy
Steiff
KNOPF IM OHR

Steiff started its replica program in 1980 with 17-inch Papa, far left in photo, which was originally produced in 1905. Following Papa, from left, was the grey Richard Steiff bear, also a 1905 replica, 12½ inches high; 12½-inch Dicky-Bear came in 1985, reproducing the 1930 bear; in 1986, the popular 1953 Jackie was reproduced, 10 inches high; and in 1991 the 1904 Bärle replica, 19¾ inches high, was created.

things possible for children. In recent decades, however, adult collectors have begun to openly share their love of Steiff. Early Steiff toys are avidly sought, and bring record prices on the secondary market, whether sold at international auctions or by antique-toy dealers. The company has responded to this growing interest by re-creating some of the classic designs. The replica program began in 1980 with the re-creation of an early teddy bear; in 1983 Richard Steiff's Bärle of 1905 was reproduced. Since 1983, the company has expanded beyond the reproduction of teddy bears. Looking to their rich archives, Steiff designers have reproduced nearly one hundred pieces, including the 1955 classic Leo lion (1984); Margarete Steiff's first felt elephant (1984–85); and the 1928 tabby cat (1986). In 1987, two felt dolls—Albert Schlopsnies' Betty the tennis player from 1913 and Gentleman in morning coat from 1914—were reproduced. Distinctive characters like the Schlopsnies 1911 Coloro the clown (1989) and the 1904 Uncle Sam (1994) have also been added to the popular replica program.

The story of Margarete Steiff's toy company does not end here; it merely begins with its past. The following pages reveal the seemingly endless variety of riches Steiff's craftspeople create today as they continue the tradition of making timeless toys.

Chapter 2

The Current Collection

or

Franzi's Journey through the World of Steiff

Once upon a time there was a small, fair-haired bear named Franzi. Like many wonderful soft toys, he came to life at the Steiff factory in Giengen, Germany.

Franzi was a young bear, but he was an adventurous dreamer. He eagerly awaited his turn to go out into the big world, for he had heard many tantalizing tales from the other Steiff teddy bears about the cheerful toy shops and warm homes where children would welcome him into their hearts. Day after day, other bears were taken from the open boxes where they rested, waiting, but Franzi was never among the chosen. One day, our young hero simply ran out of patience.

Here's Franzi now. Let him tell you his story.

Below right: Two brown otters, sitting and standing; baby otter, standing. **Opposite page:** Classic 1952 mohair elephant with felt saddlecloth; classic 1951 mohair jointed teddy bear with squeaker.

Hi, it's me, Franzi. It's true, I ran out of patience—patience is not my forte. One morning, I simply couldn't wait any longer—a whole world was out there to explore! I took matters into my own hands. I grabbed onto another teddy bear's leg and held tight when he was lifted out. Next thing I knew, we were in another box, this one with a lid that closed tight over us. I could see nothing, but felt lots of lifting, bumping and dropping. Good thing we were packed in there so tight. It seemed like forever I was in that dark, tight place, but finally I heard the unmistakable sound of the box being opened, and I was nearly blinded by the unfamiliar daylight. A pair of hands lifted me out and put me on a shelf with the other teddies. I was in the world at last!

But suddenly, the hands picked me up again. There was a big fuss among the human voices.

"Hey, what's this bear?"

"He came with the Steiffs, but he can't be a Steiff—he doesn't have the button in his ear. You know they don't let any of their animals leave that factory without the button-in-ear."

"Looks just like a Steiff, though...but we can't sell it with the others...well, put him on the shelf, he's cute, he'll sell eventually."

Not a Steiff bear? Of course I was! I didn't know *where* I was, but I certainly knew *who* I was. Back on the shelf, I looked around at the others who had come with me. Sure enough, each one had a little metal button in his left ear, with a colorful tag reading "Steiff." Surreptitiously, I felt my left ear. No button. So that was the problem—that was why they hadn't sent me out yet. Well, the next step was clear. I'd have to go home and get my button.

My decision was simple. My journey home was not. I leapt off the shelf into the world of Steiff, trusting my animal instincts to bring me home. As I searched for the factory in Giengen, I met creatures I never imagined existed. I learned that Steiff means much more than just teddies; there are many faces, many bodies, many personalities (yikes!). Often I wanted to turn back from fear or fatigue, but my mission was irrevocable. Come with me on my journey through these pages and meet some of the creatures I encountered as I wended my way through the wondrous world of Steiff.

Steiff
KNOPF IM OHR

Above: Persian cat, lying down. **Right:** Young wolf and wolf, lying down. **Far right:** Miniature1908 mohair red teddy bear; 1938 mohair panda bear replica; miniature 1908 mohair blue teddy bear.

These two offered to pull me on a sled.

KNOPF IM OHR

Original
Steiff
KNOPF IM OHR
Ginny
Steiff
KNOPF IM OHR

Left: Brown spotted guinea pig; gold hamster, sitting up; spotted Ginny guinea pig with squeaker. **Above:** Mocky hippopotamus, standing, with yellow spotted Slo tortoise on its back; two Mockili baby hippopotamuses, standing. **Following pages**, from left in photo: blond Petsy; light-brown Petsy; dark-brown Molly; light-brown Molly; light-brown Petsy; light-brown Molly.

Exercise will keep me fit during the journey.

Petsy
Petsy
Molly

They want me to stay
and join their club.
Petsy

Right: A classic 22-inch Mr. Cinnamon mohair teddy with squeaker is surrounded by smaller mohair replicas, ranging from 4 to 7 inches high. From left on floor: a blond original teddy bear replica with turnable head; 1904 cinnamon bear replica; original grey jointed teddy bear. On Mr. Cinnamon's shoulder: two miniature 1960 jointed blond teddy bears.

She's looking for Papa Bear.

Above: Three Tulla ducks (lilac/rose, brown/green and brown/yellow) with squeakers; two Biep baby ducks (lilac/rose and brown/yellow) with squeakers.

Above: Poppel rabbit, crouching. **Right:** Koala bear. **Opposite page:** Brown spotted Bertha cow, standing (rear view); Resi cow standing, with leather collar and bell; miniature Bessy cow, standing.

*Why are **you** crying?*
I'm the one who's lost.

Bessy

Above: Grey and white standing cockerel. **Right:** Black Scoty Scottish terrier with blue/black checkered scarf; white Tommi West Highland terrier with red/white checkered scarf.

Following pages: Three standing Ferdy horses, each with leather harness; Lamby lamb, lying down; standing lamb; standing Bertha cow; two standing Flocky goats.

Why would I want to go through Scotland?

Original
Lamby

Ferdy
Flocky
Flocky

Above: Miniature standing Piggy pig; two standing Wutzi wild boars; miniature standing Wutzi wild boar. **Right:** Molly pony; Floppy rabbit; Cosy Manni rabbit, sitting up; Molly donkey.

Left: Classic 1920 mohair jointed light-blond classic teddy bear with growler; light-brown teddy bear with growler.

Holding paws in public is a matter of personal taste.

Left: Beige Bongo gibbon; panda. **Above,** clockwise from left: Standing pig; three standing Piggy pigs; miniature standing Suggy pig; miniature standing Wutzi wild boar.

Okay, so bears have big heads!

Right: Classic 1935 mohair Fellow terrier with leather collar; classic 1928 tipped mohair jointed Petsy teddy bear with growler; classic 1909 mohair jointed dark-brown teddy bear with growler. **Opposite page:** Two standing Hocky dromedaries; miniature Hango orangutan, sitting behind miniature sitting Coco chimpanzee.

The camels could come in handy if the trek is much longer, but what do I do with those other guys?

Coco

Above: Floppy bear; bedtime rabbit; Cosy light-brown Hoppy rabbit; jumping. **Right:** Two classic 1920 mohair jointed teddy bears with growlers. In light-brown bear's lap: 1960 mohair jointed caramel teddy bear. In dark-brown bear's lap: 1927 mohair jointed brass Petsy. **Far right:** Standing Kiwi.

Every bear should have a little buddy.

Lamby
Steiff
KNOPF IM OHR

Opposite page: Standing Bea sheep; Lamby lamb, lying down. **Left:** Mohair jointed light-blond teddy bear with growler. **Following pages:** Grey Topsi rabbit, sitting; Dormili rabbit, sitting; beige Topsi rabbit, sitting; brown/beige Putsi rabbit, sitting; brown/beige Putsi rabbit, lying down; mustard-spotted Dormili rabbit, sitting.

She's single and wants to know if I'm married.

Steiff
KNOPF IM OHR
Steiff
KNOPF IM OHR
Dormili
Steiff
KNOPF IM OHR

Putsi
Steiff
KNOPF IM OHR

Right, clockwise from penguin: 1957 miniature mohair Peggy penguin; 1951 mohair jointed caramel/white tipped Zotty teddy bear; 1952 replica mohair Niki rabbit with growler; 1926 mohair jointed yellow teddy clown; 1926 mohair jointed rose teddy clown; 1934 miniature mohair St. Bernard with turnable head and leather collar, sitting.

He says he's King Bunny.

Left: Sissy cat, standing; miniature grey dog, standing. **Below:** Miniature elephant, standing; two Trampili baby elephants, standing.

Opposite page: Snorry fox cub, standing; brown/green drake with squeaker; Movi swan. **Left:** Molly teddy bear with dangling frog.

Original
Steiff
KNOPF IM OHR
Original
Steiff
KNOPF IM OHR
Original
Steiff
KNOPF IM OHR
Made in Germany by
Steiff
KNOPF IM OHR
Original
Steiff
KNOPF IM OHR
Made in Germany by
Steiff
KNOPF IM OHR

Above: Striped Minou cat, lying down.
Opposite page: Two blue Imperial fish and two yellow/white Pincette fish.

Original
Steiff
KNOPF IM OHR

Opposite page: Two grey/brown jumping monkeys, standing. **Left:** two spotted Robby seals with squeakers, lying down; Issy baby seal.
Following pages: Taky panther; Leo lion; Paddy leopard; Radjah tiger; tiger, standing.

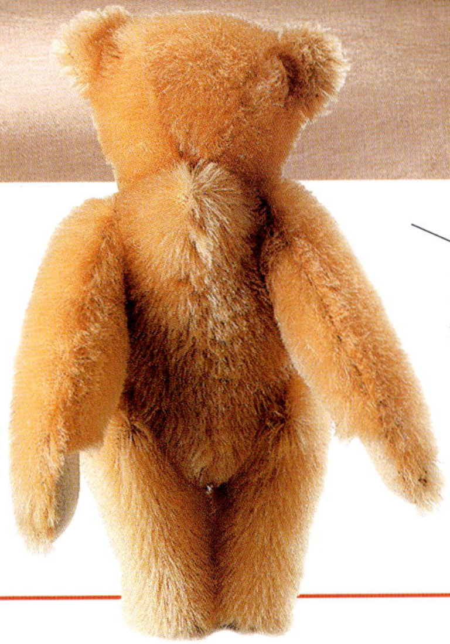

*If I turn my back,
maybe they'll stop staring.*

Steiff
KNOPF IM OHR
Steiff
KNOPF IM OHR

Yikes! Get me outta here!

Right: Grey goose and white farm goose, both standing; beige-tipped baby duck with squeaker; beige Daggi baby duck with squeaker.
Opposite page: Dalmatian with leather collar, sitting down.
Following pages: Mohair jointed teddy bear with growler dressed as a sailor; mohair jointed teddy bear with growler, dressed as chef; mohair jointed teddy bear with growler dressed as huntsman; classic 1928 mohair chow with squeaker.

This guy says there are 101 ways home.

Original
Steiff
KNOPF IM OHR
Molly
Teddy
Steiff
KNOPF IM OHR

Opposite page: Large dark-brown Molly teddy bear draws in the group: white Molly teddy bear, yellow Molly teddy bear, dark-brown Petsy teddy bear and a small beige teddy bear. **Above:** Ango puma, standing.

I don't like the way he's looking at them....

Right: Blond Ferdy horse with leather harness, standing; miniature light-brown Rocko horse, standing; miniature dark-brown Steiff Racy horse, standing. **Opposite page:** Golden brown Mümmel hare, lying down.

What's ***he*** *looking at?*

I feel naked.

Opposite page: A group of classic 1907 mohair jointed dressed teddy bears with growlers; miniature mohair bear cub with turnable head, leather collar and bell, standing; classic 1928 mohair Tabby cat on wheels, with turnable head, taffeta collar, small bell and towing rope. **Above:** Grey chinchilla; elephant; Piky porcupine. **Left:** Nagy beaver, standing; spotted Dalle guinea pig; spotted Swinny guinea pig with squeaker.

Original
Original

Opposite page: Two slender-tailed grey/beige tipped mierkats, sitting up; West American chipmunk; Kecki squirrel; standing marmot.
Left: Yellow Friedericke goose; white Pelican with bag in beak; green Froggy frog, lying down.
Following pages: Two spotted Robby seals with squeakers, lying down; Issy baby seal; Larili baby penguin.

Robby

Steiff
KNOPF IM OHR
Lenli

Above: Wittie young eagle owl and miniature Wittie young eagle owl. **Right:** Three classic 1951 mohair jointed teddy bears with squeaker, in a variety of sizes; classic 1939 mohair young lion on wheels.

Hi! Can I ride, too?

Lulac
Lulac

Opposite page: Cinnamon Lulac dangling rabbit; grey Lulac dangling rabbit; brown/white Molly goat, lying down. **Above:** Molly Schnauzer with leather collar, sitting; dangling mouse; Molly husky with leather collar, lying down.

Everybody's getting so cozy here.

I can do that one-handed!
Micki
nach Diehl-Film
Steiff
KNOPF IM OHR

The joyful Mecki hedgehog family: two Papa Meckis; two Mama Mickis; their son Macki and their daughter Mucki.

No fair! I'd rather be playing around on the floor, too.

Above: Red striped kitten, lying aside; grey striped kitten, lying aside; grey/brown Raudi dachshund with collar; red striped Whiskas cat, sitting. **Opposite page:** Xorry fox, lying down; deer, curled up; West American chipmunk; Ricky squirrel. **Following pages:** Polar bear with two baby polar bears.

Xorry
Steiff
KNOPF IM OHR
Original
Steiff
KNOPF IM OHR

CE

STEIFF-ORIGINAL
Leo
1956 - Replica

Opposite page: 1956 replica mohair Leo lion. **Left:** Golden-brown Mümmel hare, sitting; golden-brown Mümmel hare, lying down. **Above:** Grey manatee, lying down; polar bear, lying down; brown Slo tortoise.

KNOPF IM OHR

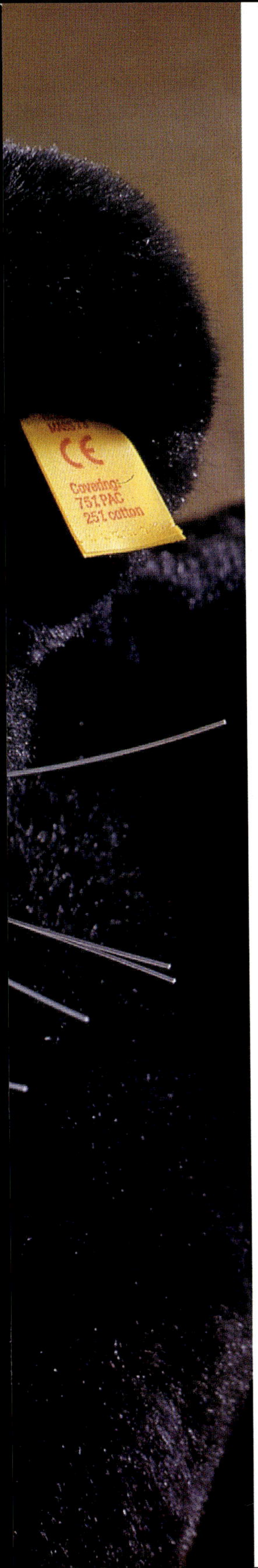

Opposite page: Jointed Petsy panda bear with squeaker; Molly young panther, lying down. **Above:** Paddy leopard, standing.

Uh oh…I can't bear to look….

Above: Two brown tipped bears, sitting. **Right:** Classic 1938 mohair bear on wooden wheels with turnable head, leather collar and rowing rope; mohair jointed Steiff growling bear; classic 1909 mohair jointed teddy bear with growler. **Following pages:** A dozen felines include: striped Snuffi cat; grey spotted savage cat, sitting; grey striped kitten, sitting; grey striped kitten, standing; red striped kitten, lying aside; grey striped kitten, lying aside; red striped Whiskas cat, sitting; Sissi cat, standing; striped Minou cat, lying down; grey cat, standing.

Stop kissing and check out that guy on wheels—I sure wish I had some.

Classic

Above: Three Piff marmots, two sitting up and one standing. **Opposite page:** Two classic 1920 mohair jointed teddy bears with growlers.

They're in love and don't remember anything.

1920

1909
Classic
Teddybär
Teddy
Baby

A grouping of teddy bears includes: 1909 classic mohair jointed teddy bear with growler; miniature mohair jointed caramel/white tipped Zotty; miniature mohair jointed Teddy-Baby with decorated leather collar and bell; jointed Petsy teddy bear; miniature mohair jointed cinnamon teddy bear; gold 4-inch mohair jointed original teddy bear; classic 1907 mohair jointed dressed teddy bear with squeaker; miniature 1953 mohair jointed Jackie.

Above: Two miniature giraffes, standing; Leo lion, standing. **Right:** 1906 Foxy Grandpa jointed felt doll replica; 1911 Musician Brown jointed felt doll replica with trumpet; 1912 Hungarian jointed felt doll replica with horse with leather saddle and bridle; 1913 baseball player jointed felt doll replica with baseball hat.

A band with a baseball player? Where am I?

Above: Grey/beige tipped slender-tailed mierkat, sitting up: two Raggy raccoons, sitting up. **Opposite page:** Ango puma, standing.

I applaud your courage also, but what are we going to do about that long-whiskered puma?

Steiff
KNOPF IM OHR

Baby Gora
Steiff
KNOPF IM OHR
Made in Germany by
Steiff
KNOPF IM OHR
Jocko
Steiff
KNOPF IM OHR

Opposite page: Jocko chimpanzee with squeaker reclines upon Gora baby gorilla with squeaker. **Above:** Two grey/brown jumping monkeys.

I need a rest, too.

Above: Classic 1928 tipped mohair jointed Petsy teddy bear with growler; classic 1909 mohair jointed teddy bear with growler. **Right:** Orca sword whale; Mobby whale; Finny dolphin with squeaker.

Only polar bears should swim with the sharks.

Finny
Steiff
KNOPF IM OHR

Original
Steiff
KNOPF IM OHR

Opposite page: Grey spotted savage cat, sitting down; Persian cat, lying down. **Above:** Three grey striped kittens, two standing and one sitting. **Left:** Dalmatian with leather collar, sitting down. **Following pages:** A menagerie of monkeys includes: miniature Bamboo gorilla; miniature Coco chimpanzee; miniature Hango orangutan; four Jocko chimpanzees, two brown, two dark brown; grey Gora baby gorilla with squeaker; two Bonbo costume monkeys.

Kittens are cute, but so dependent.

Jocko
Steiff
KNOPF IM OHR
Kocko
Jocko
Steiff
KNOPF IM OHR
Bamboo

Jocko
Steiff
KNOPF IM OHR
Baby Gora
Steiff
KNOPF IM OHR
Coco

Opposite page: Jointed Petsy teddy bear with squeaker astride a Molly camel; Molly lion. **Above:** Two Hocky dromedaries, standing; miniature Trotty dromedary, standing.

Headstands relieve tension and the desire to hibernate.

Above: Two miniature deer, standing; Moosy elk, standing; miniature stag, standing.
Opposite page: Brown tipped bear, sitting.

Steiff
KNOPF IM OHR
1927
Classic
Petsy
Made in Germany
Classic

Left: Classic 1927 mohair jointed yellow Petsy teddy bear with growler; classic 1928 mohair Tabby cat on wooden wheels with turnable head, taffeta collar, small bell and towing rope; classic 1906 mohair jointed beige teddy bear with growler; classic 1928 mohair jointed tipped Petsy teddy bear with growler; miniature 1905 mohair jointed grey Richard Steiff teddy bear. **Above:** Two Diggy moles, sitting; one skunk, standing.

I'm getting out of here before that skunk gets upset.

STEIFF-ORIGINAL-MARKE
Leo
1956 · Replica

Opposite page: 1956 mohair Leo lion replica; mohair Linda giraffe, standing; miniature 1932 mohair Leo lion replica, sitting; miniature 1951 mohair tiger with turnable head, sitting. **Above:** Sigi badger, standing; grey/brown Raudi dachshund with collar, standing.

These dogs lead a soft life.

Above: Yello fox terrier, standing; Bernie St. Bernard with leather collar, playing; Bernie St. Bernard with leather collar, lying down; Bernie St. Bernard with leather collar and little barrel, sitting. **Opposite page:** Lamb, standing; Hasso Alsatian dog with leather collar, sitting. **Following pages:** Two Taky panthers, one lying down, one standing; Coco chimpanzee, sitting.

Coco

Above: Toffy squirrel; duckbill.
Right: Grey/white cockerel; grey hen.

I don't believe the sky is falling.

Made in
KNOPF IM

Above: Two llamas. **Right:** Miniature 1905 mohair jointed Bärle teddy bear; classic 1927 mohair jointed Petsy teddy bear with growler; 1960 mohair jointed teddy bear (rear view).

Am I seeing double?

1927
Classic
Petsy
Steiff

Left: Nosy rhinoceros, standing.
Above: Striped Snuffi cat, sitting.

KNOPF IM OHR

Left: Young wolf and wolf, lying down.
Above: Standing Joggi hedgehog; two Joggi hedgehogs, sitting up.

I think I've spotted the right direction!

Now I'm picking up the scent…of Steiff.

Above: Two Karro brown bears, sitting; miniature Browny bear, standing. **Right:** Joggi hedgehog, sitting up; Toffy squirrel.

Made in Germany by Steiff ®
KNOPF IM OHR
Joggi
Steiff ®
KNOPF IM OHR

Made in Germany by
Steiff
KNOPF IM OHR

Opposite page: Golden-brown Mümmel hare; lying down; two Dormili rabbits, sitting. **Above:** Issy polar bear; two spotted Robby seals with squeakers; miniature Wally walrus; miniature Lommy polar bear; Clippy dolphin.

Maybe if I click my heels three times and say "There's no place like home"—

Brummbär
Steiff
KNOPF IM OHR
Teddy Baby
Teddy Baby

Opposite page: Miniature mohair bear cub with turnable head, leather collar and bell; mohair jointed Steiff growling bear with growler; two miniature 1930 mohair Teddy-Baby bears with decorated collars and bells; miniature 1953 mohair jointed Jackie. **Left:** Molly young panther; Molly zebra, two jointed Petsy panda bears with squeakers.

—Hey, it's beginning to look familiar around here!

Right: Three Slo tortoises, green, brown spotted and yellow spotted. **Far right:** Two Kango kangaroos with babies in pouches; two miniature Kango kangaroos; Yuku miniature koala.

Hooray! It worked! And I know I can beat ***those*** *guys to the factory door!*

Kango
Yuku

Yes, I made it! I reached home at last and waited patiently among my fellow teddies for my turn with the button lady. Boy—wait until my friends see me! Now, wherever I go, everybody will know I'm a Steiff!

Please turn the page to take a visit to Franzi's home, the Margarete Steiff factory in Giengen, where no animal is allowed to leave without a button-in-ear!

Snorry
Robby
Biep
Biep

Chapter 3

How the Toys are Made

The process of creating a soft toy has not changed dramatically since the days when the Steiff family walked the floors of the workshop in Giengen. There are certainly many more workers involved, and many more animals produced. Today, about five hundred people work at the factory in Giengen, half of them in the sewing department.

Design

The production process is set into motion when the design team receives an assignment to create a new animal. Eight designers gather to brainstorm through the proposal stage, considering how the piece should be constructed, which materials and stuffing will be used, and what color and size the finished animal will be. The design department is responsible for creating more than two hundred new toys every year, and often the designers look for inspiration in the extensive archives, which hold a complete collection of toys made from the days of Margarete Steiff until today. This remarkable research source, organized alphabetically by types of animals, takes up two long rooms, lined with row after row of open shelves. One room holds toys made prior to World War II; the second room is filled with post-war creations.

Once a rough idea of the proposed piece is agreed upon, a prototype is made for viewing by other key departments and the top management. If the decision is made to produce the toy, a hand sample is created, from which calculations as to materials and cost are determined. Then technical designers take their turn, planning production procedures, plotting out the actual engineering and construction of the animal, and deciding what new tools must be bought or created for the production of the toy. Every new design needs some new tools, whether it be knives

Left, above, opposite and preceding pages: Designing a new animal involves a team of designers and technical designers who work from sketches, books and actual materials as they consider how the piece should be constructed and which fabrics and stuffing will be used. **Inset, preceding pages:** Dies are just one of the methods employed at Steiff for cutting pattern pieces.

for cutting the material, stencils for painting, or patterns for any screen painting that must be done on the plush. Normally, the entire production process to bring a new toy into existence takes four to five months, although occasionally, if there is an urgent rush for a new animal, it can be completed in two weeks.

Above and right: Once a new piece has been designed, a prototype is created for further consideration. The felt pieces that make up this new elephant for the Steiff Club, above, were created from the paper patterns at right, which are shown with an early Steiff catalog featuring the original version of the elephant.

KNOPF IM OHR

Left: Dies are used for cutting out patterns for animals that are made from short plush, or from fabrics without fur. The company has a large collection of dies, but new ones are often required for new designs.
Above: Numerous pattern pieces, labeled as to animal and body part, hang in the factory, ready for production.

Cutting

The technical designers break down the animal into pattern pieces, which are cut out, using dies or screen printing, depending on the thickness of the fabric. If the designated plush is more than a half-inch thick, the patterns are printed by screen on the back of the plush, and cut out by hand, using a procedure very much like stenciling. Dies are used for short plush and all fabrics without fur.

Above: A cutter uses the die method, being careful to make the most efficient use of fabric and leave no waste. **Right:** Row upon row of colorful fabrics is a common sight at the factory in Giengen. This bright array is a selection of wool felts.

Left and above: Thicker plush is cut by another method, that of screen printing. Here the screen, which is placed on the back of the plush, is being prepared for printing. The procedure resembles that of stenciling; the fabric is placed under a screen, which has been perforated by a pattern. The color seeps through the perforation, leaving the pattern on the fabric, which is then cut out by hand.
Following pages: A vast array of patterned fur hangs in wait. The pieces will soon be shaped into playful creatures.

Above: A worker considers the printed screens. **Right:** The screen printing leaves a clear pattern on the fabric, which the careful cutter follows closely. **Far right:** Paper pattern pieces, properly labeled, are always ready for use. When a new design is approved, however, new patterns must often be created.

Sewing and Jointing

The prepared pieces then go to the sewing department, where the designer instructs the seamstresses as to the correct order for putting them together. All the seamstresses at the factory undergo six months of extensive training by the head of the sewing department before they are allowed to work on any of the toys. Each one learns to specialize in certain animals and eventually develops a

repertoire of thirty to forty designs.

In some cases, a seamstress might make an entire animal, but more often, one sews the limbs while another sews the heads and bodies. The sewing is a slow, careful process, done centimeter by centimeter. When working with mohair plush, the seamstresses must also constantly check the color of the plush, which can vary from dye lot to dye lot. Mohair plush is difficult to dye, and often

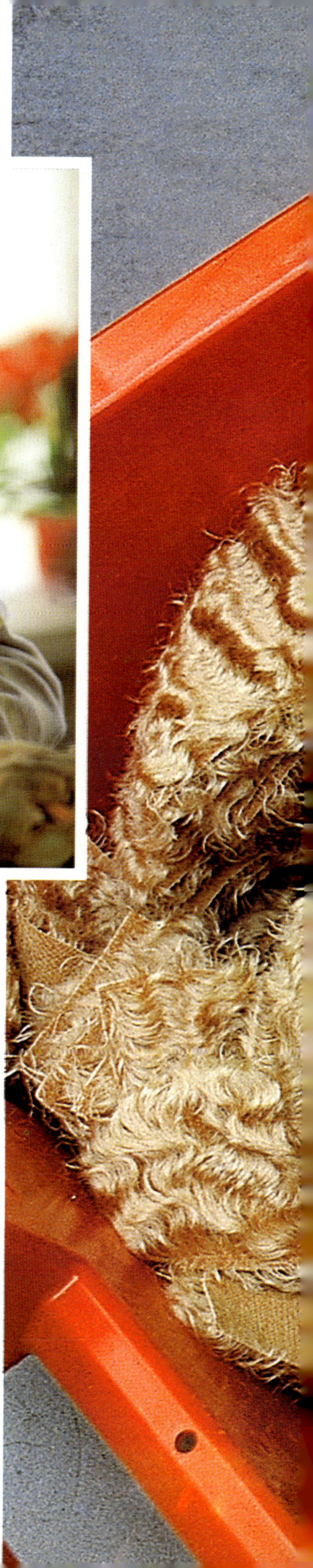

Right: Once they have been cut, the pattern pieces go to the sewing department. **Left and above:** There, trained seamstresses begin the process of putting the pieces together to form the animal. The designer of a new toy always instructs the seamstresses who will be responsible for the animal as to the correct sewing procedure for each new animal that enters their repertoires.

there are variations. It's important to properly match the mohair pieces on a single animal, so that the animal is one consistent color. During the sewing process, the head of the sewing department performs what the company calls a "flying control"—she goes to each table and checks to make sure each seamstress is sewing properly.

Above: Sewing is the most time-consuming part of toy production. Once all the pieces of a new toy have been sewn, turned, joined and jointed, the toy is ready for the next phase, the stuffing process, to begin. **Right:** Racks filled with a seemingly endless variety of fabrics are everywhere at the Steiff factory.
Following pages: One step closer to completion: stuffed animal parts await the next phase of production.

The pieces are sewn with the wrong sides together, and must then be turned so that the right side is on the outside. The head and limbs are now joined to the body, and if joints are required, they are inserted at this point. The joints are simple constructions, as they were in Richard Steiff's day. A metal pin is inserted into the limb, then a cardboard disc is placed at either end of the pin to hold it. The discs are glued to the fabric to secure the joint. Once sewn, turned, joined and jointed, the piece is ready for stuffing—or, if it is a soft toy, for eye insertion.

Steiff uses two methods of eye placement, depending upon the requirements for the type of piece being produced. All the soft toys must have safety eyes, which must be inserted before stuffing, from the inside of the head. These eyes are backed with a nail and a safety disc that hold the eye firmly in place so that a young child cannot remove it. The classic method is used for the hard stuffed animals: once the animal is stuffed, the eyes are stitched onto the head with thread.

Stuffing

A variety of stuffings are used at Steiff, depending on the kind of animal being made. The classic mohair pieces are stuffed with wood shavings, as are the replicas. The softer, floppy animals are stuffed with polyester, polyurethane foam or acrylic fiber. Pieces with long arms and legs are more likely to be stuffed with foam than with fiber, since fiber has a tendency to roll around in the body. It is easier to control the hardness or softness of the foam pieces as they are being stuffed into the toy.

Once the toy has been sewn, jointed and stuffed, the final seam is closed and the animal goes to its first official quality-control checkpoint. Here, all the seams are checked and then, if they are shown to have been done properly, are stretched out. The fur is brushed so that it is all standing outside the seamlines.

Left, above and right: The size and shape of the animal dictates the type of stuffing it will have. Replicas, like the record teddy bears being stuffed at left, and other mohair classics, like the teddy bear being stuffed at right, are filled with wood shavings known as excelsior, which have been used since the earliest days of production. Soft animals, as well as larger ones, like the studio bear above, are stuffed with polyester fibers.

Opposite page and left: Studio-size classic animals like these giraffes and the popular cartoon character Mecki, which require firm bodies, are also stuffed with excelsior—a physically demanding job when such a large piece is in the works. **Above:** Special stuffing tools, like those shown with these record teddy bear replicas, help the process along.

Finishing

Now sewn, joined, jointed and stuffed, the animal is ready for the finishing details. The nose and paws are stitched, any claws or other accessories are added, and the piece travels to a second quality-control checkpoint, where the stitching and eyes are checked. The checker ensures that the eyes are symmetrical and, most importantly, that no holes have been made in the fabric where the nose and paws have been stitched, and that no stuffing is coming out.

Finally, the animal is checked against the original hand sample. If it passes the comparison test, it is ready to receive the legendary button-in-ear. A special machine inserts a shiny new button, inscribed with the word "Steiff," and the proper cloth tag, in the left ear of each new animal. Now unmistakably identifiable as a Steiff creation, the toy animal is ready to leave its home in Giengen and make its way to a toy shop somewhere in the world, where it will wait for just the right child to come and claim it for his or her very own special companion.

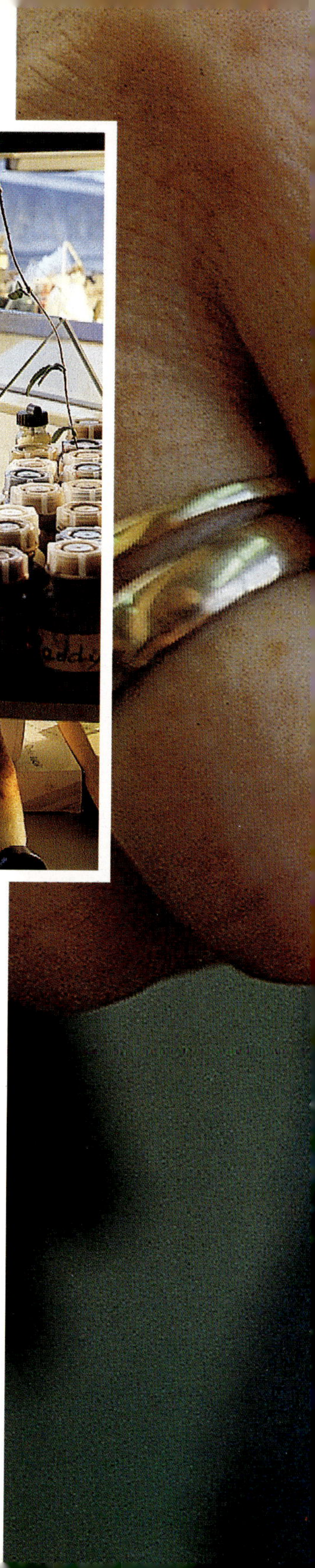

Left, above and right: The final stages of production include finishing details, such as nose and paw stitching, and painting, as well as the addition of any accessories, such as claws or decorative features.

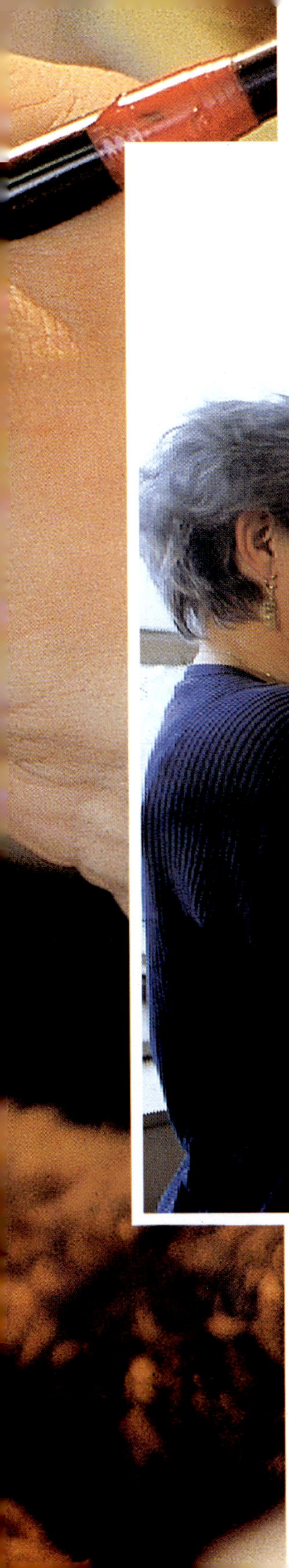

Left: Animals that require painting, like this bear, wait until all other details have been completed before they receive these final finishes. **Above:** After a final pass through quality control, the completed toys line up patiently, like the huskies above, to receive their button-in-ear.

Opposite page and left: When the animal has successfully passed through all of its quality-control checkpoints, including the check against the original hand sample, it is ready to receive its button-in-ear, which identifies it as a Steiff creation.
Above: Then, it's off into the world!

STEIFF CIRCUS
LEO
STEIFF
CIRCUS
FIGHTING
LIONS
STEIFF
WILD ANIMALS
86

Chapter 4

Steiff in America

Since the beginning of this century, strong ties between the United States and Steiff have inspired imaginative toys and gifts created especially for North America. Today's exclusively American pieces, more numerous than ever, continue to celebrate the rich enduring collaborative tradition between this venerable German company and the American popular culture.

The history of Steiff's relationship with the United States dates back to 1902, when Margarete Steiff first sent her nephew Paul to New York to promote the sale of Steiff toys in North America. Since that time, the United States has always been an important source of sales for the toy company, but there is much more to the enduring connection than just economics. From the start, American culture has also been an important source of inspiration for Steiff designers.

Preceding pages: The circus wagon limited edition set was sold exclusively by Reeves International beginning in 1986. The Steiff animals were in circus wagons designed by Reeves and produced elsewhere. The elephant on wheels led the circus calliope in 1986; the circus wagon cage with the lying lion in it was produced in 1987; the circus wagon with the giraffe followed in 1988; the circus wagon with the tiger was made in 1989; the last piece in the set was the circus wagon with two bears in 1990.

Above: In the early years of this century, Steiff workers used excelsior as stuffing for the animals. The material is still used in some animals today.

The ties have been strong throughout the twentieth century, but the relationship between the United States and Steiff took a new direction in the decade of the 1980s, when the company began to produce toys exclusively for sale in North America in greater numbers than ever before. Records of toys made exclusively for sale in North America before 1980 are sparse, but over the past seventeen years collector interest in these exclusives has inspired several publications on the subject. Today there are several excellent sources of detailed records. (See bibliography on page 222.) The company itself has samples of North American exclusives produced since 1913 in its comprehensive archives at the factory in Giengen. But let's go back to the beginning of the twentieth century and take a look at the development of the relationship between Steiff and the North American continent.

In 1903, when Paul Steiff arrived in New York, his mandate was to actively promote the sale of Steiff toys in the U.S.A., and his first step was to establish a showroom at 640 Broadway. Being a meticulous record keeper, he maintained a careful journal of toy shipments and sales. From his records, we know that in February 1903 a large container holding five wooden crates of the most recent toy samples arrived in New York and that among these was the company's first jointed bear: Bär 55 PB. The early introduction of the bear in New York was not successful, as is well known by now. Even the order for three thousand bears placed by Hermann Berg, the toy buyer for American importer George Borgfeldt, at the Leipzig Spring Fair a month later in March 1903 had no lasting impact. (Those bears disappeared into the United States marketplace without leaving a trace.) Paul disappointedly returned to Germany after fifteen months, having made no significant inroads.

But in 1904, when Margarete sent another nephew, Franz, to the St. Louis World's Fair with the smaller, improved Bär 35 PB, the venture had a much happier result. The lighter, more appealing bear succeeded where the first had failed—in winning American hearts and garnering attention and awards for the company. Steiff also created a stunning display for the entrance to the Toy Exhibition Hall: a triple archway with twenty-four clowns and two police dolls. The dolls were an imposing thirty-

nine inches high. That year Steiff won the Grand Prix medal at the World's Fair and gold medals were awarded to Margarete and Richard Steiff. The year was an economic success, too; Steiff sold twelve thousand bears in 1904.

The dolls created for the World's Fair were larger versions of Steiff's new comic felt dolls, introduced, with great success, that same year. Many of the most successful dolls were inspired by American cartoon characters, starting with Foxy Grandpa, Foxy Boy, Happy Hooligan and The Katzenjammer Kids. Eventually Buster Brown and Johnny Gruelle's Mr. Twee Deedle were added to the collection and, in 1919, Barney Google and Spark Plug. Also popular in the original 1904 collection were American characters like Uncle Sam, and fat and thin varieties of American policemen. Later the company turned to American children's books for inspiration, and created figures like Mother Hubbard in 1909. (The character was unknown in Germany, so there Steiff sold her as the witch from the fairy tale of *Hansel and Gretel*.)

In the 1920s Felix the Cat became a popular American

In the 1950s the Loucap Company competed with Reeves International for representation of Steiff in the United States. These dinosaurs were available exclusively from Loucap. Clockwise from the left foreground they are: tyrannosaurus, 1958; brontosaurus, 1958; dinosaurus, 1958; dinosaurier, 1959.

Below: Steiff made some pieces in the 1950s for the United States military and naval academies, such as these goats and mules. From left, they are: Navy goat, 1957; Navy goat, 1960; Army mule, 1957; velvet Army mule, 1957.

Right: This goat was designed for the United States Navy in 1954.

comic-strip and silent-movie star. In 1927, George Borgfeldt, by then the company's sole agent in the United States and thus a vitally important link between the firm and the United States market, asked Steiff to create a Felix prototype. Although Paul Steiff believed that Felix would not be successful because black-and-white characters were too difficult to sell, Steiff reproduced the popular cat. However, Paul's prediction turned out to be accurate; only 605 examples of Felix were made.

A much more successful introduction, and one that heralded an important Steiff relationship for the future, was Walt Disney's Mickey Mouse, who first appeared on the screen in 1929. In 1930 Paul Steiff saw his first Mickey Mouse film in Stuttgart and was won over by the lively mouse. Happily for Steiff, Walt Disney had sold all the commercial rights for Mickey Mouse to George Borgfeldt, so the German company had no problem in obtaining the rights to create a felt Mickey. The mouse was produced in six sizes in 1931 and was followed, in 1932, by his companion Minnie Mouse.

The successful Disney connection was emblematic of George Borgfeldt's importance to Steiff. For many years, Borgfeldt served as the company's sole agent in the United States. Located at 16th Street and Irving Place in Manhattan, he was an important figure in the toy industry in the early years of this century. In addition to his strong representation of Steiff and other European companies, he established relationships between artists, designers and manufacturers in this country and abroad, and brought the resulting works to the United States. He had a

keen eye for innovative toys of high quality and a finger on the pulse of the American toy-buying public. Executives at Steiff today believe that not only Felix the Cat, but many of the company's early cartoon characters were initiated by Borgfeldt. His 1913 Steiff catalog, for example, included several American-oriented subjects, such as an American baseball player as well as a cowboy, an Indian and Mr. Twee Deedle.

Today it is well known that many of Steiff's creations are bought by adults, both by collectors for themselves and as gifts for other adults. As early as 1913, however, the company was already making pieces exclusive to the United States that were clearly geared to a customer long past childhood. That year felt soccer players wearing shorts, sweaters, socks and shoes, and known as the American Kickers were produced. The sweaters could be

A felt figure with a latex face, representing a devil and bearing the letter "D" for Duke University was made in 1954. He is feeding a 1952 tiger, probably created as a Princeton University mascot, even though he bears no letter "P."

In the 1950s Steiff created several university mascots, including from their archives, from left: a bull dog with a red blanket and the letter "B," possibly representing Brown University; a bulldog with a blue blanket and the letter "Y," representing Yale University; a tiger with a dark-green blanket (and smaller than the tiger in the photo on page 211) and the letter "P" representing Princeton.

ordered in navy blue with a "Y" for Yale University; in burgundy with an "H" for Harvard; in orange or black with a "P" for Princeton; and in light blue with a "C" for Columbia University. (A matching plush ball could also be bought.) Steiff's archives also hold a few animals from the 1950s known to have been made as American university mascots, as well as for the United States military and naval academies. The university mascots include a tiger wearing a dark-green blanket with a white "P" on it made in 1958 for Princeton University and two bulldogs made in 1957. One bulldog wears a light-blue blanket with a white "Y" standing for Yale University, while the other wears a red blanket with a white "B," possibly representing Brown University. The archives also hold a larger unclothed tiger dating from 1952, believed to have been made for Princeton University and a felt figure with a pitchfork tail and a latex face, representing a devil, clothed in dark blue and bearing a white "D" on its chest, made in 1954 for North Carolina's Duke University.

Two goats and two mules can also be found in Steiff's archives, and are identified as having been made exclusively for the United States military and naval academies.

The goats wear dark-blue blankets bearing a white "N"; the smaller goat dates from 1957 and the larger from 1960. Both mules date from 1957; the smaller one is velvet and wears a black blanket with the letter "A." The larger one wears a gold blanket without any letter on it.

From the early 1950s until 1992, Steiff was represented in the United States by Reeves International. Until the mid-1960s, Reeves competed for Steiff sales with two other distributors, all of whom sold the same pieces to the same shops. Reeves' primary competition came from the Ridgewood, New Jersey, Loucap Company, and in an effort to ease that competition, Steiff gave each distributor one exclusive line. Loucap was given a collection of dinosaurs, while Reeves was given a collection of trophy heads, which were animal heads mounted on wooden backgrounds, meant to serve as a decoration for a child's room.

In the mid-1960s, Reeves was given the exclusive distributorship of Steiff pieces in the United States. Many department stores with significant toy departments, however, still bought toys directly from Steiff in Germany, often attending the annual Nuremberg Toy Fair to make their orders. Often a buyer from a department store would also purchase a unique display piece made by Steiff for their Nuremberg display, which was then featured in the store's toy display. In this way, unique Steiff

Above: Reeves International distributed these two unicorns in 1983. Made exclusively for the United States, they were each available in an edition limited to 2,000, along with a lying tiger in two sizes and a lying boxer.

Left: This elephant in the Steiff archives is known to have been made exclusively for the United States in 1954. The Dalmatian was made in 1963; F.A.O. Schwarz dressed it in a red cape and crown and sold it as a store exclusive.

Above: The first pieces made exclusively for the United States after Steiff took over distribution in this country include, from left: Louis, edition of 3,500, 1994; Compass Rose, edition of 3,500, 1995; Otto, edition of 5,000, 1992; Alice, edition of 5,000, 1993. Compass Rose was created as a tribute to the first all-women's team in the America's Cup races.

Right: Forever Friends was Steiff's 1996 exclusive piece for the United States. The nine-inch pair was limited to an edition of 4,000.

items found their way into the United States market.

While the notion of exclusive pieces made for toy shops had not yet come into popularity, major stores did request special pieces from Steiff. The legendary toy store F.A.O. Schwarz often created their own exclusive sets by taking a standard Steiff toy and putting it together with other pieces from other makers. For example, in 1963 the store bought a Steiff Dalmatian, dressed it in a red velvet cape and a crown and sold it as a store exclusive.

In the 1950s and 1960s, the sale of Steiff toys in the United States was thriving. Germany's post-war economy and the devaluation of the German mark made it difficult for Steiff to sell a significant amount of toys in its native country. The United States was vitally important to the company's growth in those decades, and Steiff produced many pieces with American buyers in mind. But as the German market slowly strengthened, Steiff began looking homeward. The designs and fabrics evolved away from the classic, hard mohair animals that were so popular in the United States and towards softer, floppier animals beloved by German children in that era. In the 1970s the

balance shifted dramatically; catalogs for the United States grew thin and German sales soared.

A new, solid direction for the future was set in 1980, when executives at Steiff decided to celebrate the company's one hundredth anniversary by reproducing the mohair Papa Bear of 1903. They produced eleven thousand bears, and sent five thousand to the United States. Those five thousand bears came close to selling out upon their introduction at the 1980 American International Toy Fair. Most of them went immediately to American collectors, who were hungry for the classic Steiff bears.

The success of Papa Bear inspired further replicas, significantly expanding Steiff's production of the classic mohair animals that American collectors sought so eagerly. A second major step in this direction was taken in 1982 when The Margaret Woodbury Strong Museum in Rochester, New York, reopened, and curators asked Steiff to make a replica of one of the Steiff bears in the museum. The Margaret Strong Bear Set of four bears in chocolate brown was introduced in an edition of 2,000 limited to the United States in 1983. At the set's introduction at New York's Toy Fair, the original bear from the museum's collection was displayed alongside the replica set.

Left: For the 1991 Walt Disney World Teddy Bear Convention, Steiff produced Mickey Bear, wearing a porcelain mask and limited to an edition of 1,500. The next year, a 1,500-piece edition of Minnie Bear followed. Teddy Donald, limited to 2,500, joined them in 1993.

Below: Winnie the Pooh, center, was Steiff's limited edition of 2,500 pieces for the 1994 Disney Convention. Baloo, from *The Jungle Book*, was created in 1995 in an edition of 2,500, while a 1,500-piece edition of Gepetto Bear and Pinocchio was made in 1996.

Above: The legendary toy store F.A.O. Schwarz has a long history of working with Steiff on exclusive pieces. The polar bear, in an edition of 1,000, was exclusive to the store in 1995, while the toy musical soldier was a 1996 exclusive, limited to 2,000 pieces.

Right: The Toy Store in Toledo, Ohio, has been working with Steiff on exclusive pieces since 1987. In 1995 Golli G and Teddy B were produced in an edition of 1,500, and in 1996 Steiff created its only girl golliwogg: Molli Golli and Peg, a four-inch, fully jointed wooden peg doll, were made in a limited edition of 2,500.

Like the 100th-anniversary Papa Bear replica, the Margaret Strong bears spurred the replica production along. Reeves International designed numerous dressed versions of the Margaret Strong bears, ordering them unclothed in certain sizes and colors and then, upon their arrival, costuming them. The bears were dressed as: a Bride and Groom (1984); a Ring Bear-er and a Flower Bear-er (1985); Santa (1985); a Christening Bear (1986); a Victorian Girl and Boy (1986); a Victorian Lady and Gentleman (1987); St. Nicholas (1987); Santa's Elf (1988).

In addition to the Strong bears, Reeves created many exclusive sets in which they paired Steiff bears with other items they represented. An especially popular series was the nursery rhymes, including: Goldilocks, designed by the artist Suzanne Gibson, put together with three Steiff bears; Mary Had A Little Lamb, which paired the artist's doll and a Steiff lamb; and Little Red Riding Hood, which included a wolf mask made by Steiff to be worn by the grandmother doll.

The circus theme, associated with Steiff since the company's early years, was also explored by Reeves International. The circus train series, created between 1986 and 1990, was one of the most sought-after of all the Reeves exclusives. The set consisted of miniature Steiff animals in colorful wooden circus wagons. In 1989, the company offered a group of Steiff animals dressed as circus characters: the baby elephant became a balloon

seller; a Teddy-Baby was the ringmaster; the hippo became the Fat Lady; a chimp rode a unicycle; and a seal played with a ball. The creativity Reeves employed in developing United States exclusives was reminiscent of the way in which the American department stores of the 1950s and 1960s created their own exclusive editions, combining pieces from several popular makers.

Through the 1980s the demand for Steiff in the United States grew strong again. In 1992, executives at the company decided it was time to once again have their own headquarters in this country. Since that year Steiff has maintained their own very active Steiff USA division. In 1993, the company started the Steiff Club for collectors. Members receive a quarterly newsletter and the opportunity to acquire exclusive editions created for club members only and to participate in club activities.

Concurrent with all these developments, the Disney connection has remained rich and vital since Paul Steiff first fell in love with Mickey Mouse in 1930. In the 1950s Steiff made soft versions of Bambi and other animal characters from Disney films. Beginning in 1988, and continuing today, Steiff has produced some of its most innovative pieces for the annual Doll and Teddy Bear Conventions held for collectors at Disney World in Florida and, earlier, in Disneyland in California. In addition to exclusive bears like the charcoal-colored Teddy Baby made in 1990 for the Walt Disney World convention

Left: Especially created for the designer Ralph Lauren's Home Collection, these two bears wear distinctive Lauren clothing. The 1994 Ranch Bear in jeans and the 1993 American Bear in his signature Ralph Lauren sweater, were each limited to an edition of 3,500.

Below: A grouping of 1996 exclusive editions, each limited to 500, includes, from left: Wiggins, 13½ inches, for the Teddy Bear Museum of Naples, Florida; Casey, 12 inches, for Campbell's Collectibles of Crown Point, Indiana; The Buccaneer, 12 inches, for Fairy Tales of Lombard, Illinois.

Above: Percussion, left, and Coal are part of a series of limited edition Christmas ornaments made by Steiff and introduced at the Doll & Teddy Bear Expo held by Collector Communications Corporation in 1995 (Coal) and 1996. Each one was limited to 3,500.

Right: For the Collectors United Gathering in 1995 Steiff made the smaller bear wearing a hand-knit sweater with the organization's initials. The larger Olympian bear was made for the group's 1996 Gathering, in tribute to Collectors United's base in Atlanta, Georgia, home of that year's Olympic Games.

and the second annual teddy bear classic—a gold-colored musical that plays "When You Wish Upon a Star" made in 1993 for Disneyland—Steiff has transformed famous characters like Mickey and Minnie Mouse and Donald Duck into Mickey Bear, Minnie Bear (made for the 1991 and 1992 Walt Disney World Teddy Bear Convention and limited to 1,500 each) and Teddy Donald (made in 1993 for Walt Disney World in an edition of 2,500). While Mickey and Minnie remain almost-traditional teddy bears with masks to effect their transformations, Teddy Donald is an extraordinary creation that somehow maintains both the essence of bear-ness and the essence of duck-ness. Winnie the Pooh, of course, did not need to be transformed when he was Steiff's exclusive for the 1994 Walt Disney World Convention, nor did the 1995 Walt Disney World exclusive, Baloo, the popular character from *The Jungle Book*.

The American demand for exclusive Steiff pieces has grown dramatically in the past decade. The company has continued its strong relationship with F.A.O. Schwarz, producing at least one exclusive annually for the prestigious toy shop. Among the most recent pieces are a white polar bear in 1995 and a musical toy soldier in 1996. Steiff has produced numerous exclusives for individual shops, including a large number made since 1987 for The Toy Store (originally Hobby Center

Toys) in Toledo, Ohio. In addition to exclusive bears for The Toy Store, notable pieces made include a golliwogg holding a tiny teddy bear, Golli G & Teddy B, made in 1995 in an edition of 1,500, and a companion girl golliwogg (the only one Steiff has ever made) holding her own four-inch peg wooden doll, Molly Golli & Peg, made in an edition of 2,500 in 1996. Continuing the museum connection, Steiff made Wiggins, in a red-striped 1920s swimsuit, wearing a medallion with a map of Florida, for the Teddy Bear Museum of Naples in Florida in 1996.

Demand for Steiff exclusives has come from an ever-widening circle. Beginning in 1991, Steiff created several exclusive bears for the American fashion designer Ralph Lauren's Home Collection. All wear unmistakable Lauren ensembles: the 1994 Ranch Bear wears denim jeans and a matching jacket while the 1993 American Bear wears the signature Ralph Lauren navy-blue sweater with an American flag. In addition to entering the world of high fashion, Steiff has consistently created special pieces for events such as the Doll & Teddy Bear Expo, sponsored by Collector Communications, beginning in 1994, and the Collectors' United conventions in 1995 and 1996. The tele-

Left: Rough Rider, left, and the Berryman Bear were sold exclusively by the QVC television shopping network in 1996, and limited to 1,906 and 7,500, respectively.

Below: Boggy Creek Bob, left, was created by Steiff in 1996 to benefit Florida's new Boggy Creek Gang Camp for children with life-threatening diseases. He is 13½ inches high and was limited to an edition of 2,500. Ten percent of all sales of Bob were donated to the Boggy Creek Gang Camp. The Fisherman was a 1996 Disney edition of 1,000.

Right: Edith The Lonely Doll has a 7-inch Steiff mohair Jackie as her companion, Little Bear. Created in 1996 exclusively for The Toy Shoppe in Richmond, Virginia, Little Bear and Edith, a 14-inch felt doll by Haut Melton, came with an authorized doll-size version of their story, *The Lonely Doll* by Dare Wright. The set was limited to an edition of 750 pieces.

Below: The Passport Bear is a 1997 North American exclusive made in an edition of 3,500.

vision shopping network QVC sold Rough Rider and the Berryman Bear in 1996 while Steiff's own Collectors Club has offered exclusive editions since its inception in 1993. The company is especially proud of its 1996 association with The Boggy Creek Gang Camp, an Orlando, Florida, non-profit camping center for children with life-threatening illnesses. Modeled after Paul Newman's Hole in the Wall Gang Camp in Connecticut, the Boggy Creek Gang Camp was co-founded by Newman, General H. Norman Schwarzkopf, Theodore Forstmann and Jim and Jan Moran and opened in June 1996. To celebrate the opening, Steiff created Boggy Creek Bob, a 13½-inch jointed black bear cub. Dressed for camp, with the official Boggy Creek logo on his tee shirt, Bob was made in an edition of 2,500; Steiff donated ten percent of all sales to the Florida camp.

Most recently, Steiff has created several pieces that celebrate uniquely American stories and characters. In 1996 The Toy Shoppe in Richmond, Virginia, obtained a license from the writer/photographer Dare Wright to create in felt her fictional character of Edith, The Lonely Doll. In the 1950s Wright had told Edith's story in a series of books illustrated by black-and-white photographs. Edith's constant companion was Little Bear, clearly represented in the photographs by a tiny Jackie bear (with his button-in-ear removed). To accompany the highly realistic Edith, fashioned by Iowa felt dollmakers Kent and Martha Melton, Steiff adapted the Jackie bear pattern to a unique seven-inch size to make an equally realistic Little Bear. The playful pair was sold in an edition limited to 750 exclusively by The Toy Shoppe.

Far left: Bugs Bunny is a 1997 exclusive creation for Warner Brothers. Made in an edition of 2,500 pieces, the American cartoon legend is made of mohair with jointed limbs. He has a felt carrot, white felt gloves and teeth and stands 16½ inches high.

Left: Reggie is headed on a safari. The 1997 North American exclusive is limited to a two-year production, and is a replica of an old bear that went to Africa on a safari and kept a journal of his adventures. He has his own published journal, entitled *Safari*, backpack and proper costuming.

Other North American exclusives in 1997 were Reggie, a replica of an old bear who went to Africa on a safari, and the Passport Bear, with his own leather suitcase. Reggie's journal, entitled *Safari*, contains the story of his adventures; he also has a backpack and proper safari clothing.

An important North American exclusive in 1997 was Bugs Bunny, made for sale only in Warner Brothers Gallery Stores. The popular American cartoon character was made in mohair with felt gloves and buck teeth and holding a felt carrot, in an edition of 2,500. His arms and legs are jointed, and he stands 16½ inches high. Bugs joins the Steiff community of popular American icons like Donald Teddy, Mickey and Minnie Bear in a continuation of the rich collaborative tradition between this fine German toy company and the evolving American popular culture.

Bibliography

Cieslik, Jürgen and Marianne. *Button-in-Ear*, Jülich, Germany: Marianne Cieslik Verlag, 1989. German- and English-language editions.

_______. *Steiff-Teddy Bears: Love for a Lifetime*, Jülich, Germany: Verlag Marianne Cieslik, 1994. German- and English-language editions.

Consalvi, Peter, Sr. *Collector Steiff Values*, Grantsville, Maryland: Hobby House Press, Inc., 1994. English-language edition only.

_______. *2nd Collector Steiff Values*, Grantsville, Maryland: Hobby House Press, Inc., 1996. English-language edition only.

Pfeiffer, Gunther. *Steiff Sortiment: 1947-1995*, Taunusstein, Germany: Gunther Pfeiffer, 1995. German-language edition only.

Pistorius, Christel and Rolf. *Steiff Sensational Teddy Bears, Animals & Dolls*, Grantsville, Maryland, Hobby House Press, Inc., 1991. German- and English-language editions.

Acknowledgements

We are grateful to all who have helped in the preparation of this book, especially Falk Thomas, Jörg Junginger and Manuela Lanzinger at Margarete Steiff GmbH in Giengen, Germany, and James Maccario and Barbara Sprenger at Steiff USA in New York.

We would also like to thank all those who shared their expertise and information with us, and those who loaned photographs or pieces for photography, especially: Dick Frantz; Jim Holland; Kent and Martha Melton of Haut-Melton; Fran Ruggles of Bearaphernalia; Beth and Ben Savino of The Toy Store; and Danny and Barry Shapiro of The Toy Shoppe and European Artist Dolls.

Thanks are also due to Charley Spektor for copy-editing and production work, and to Sean Konecky of William Konecky Associates for the production of this book.